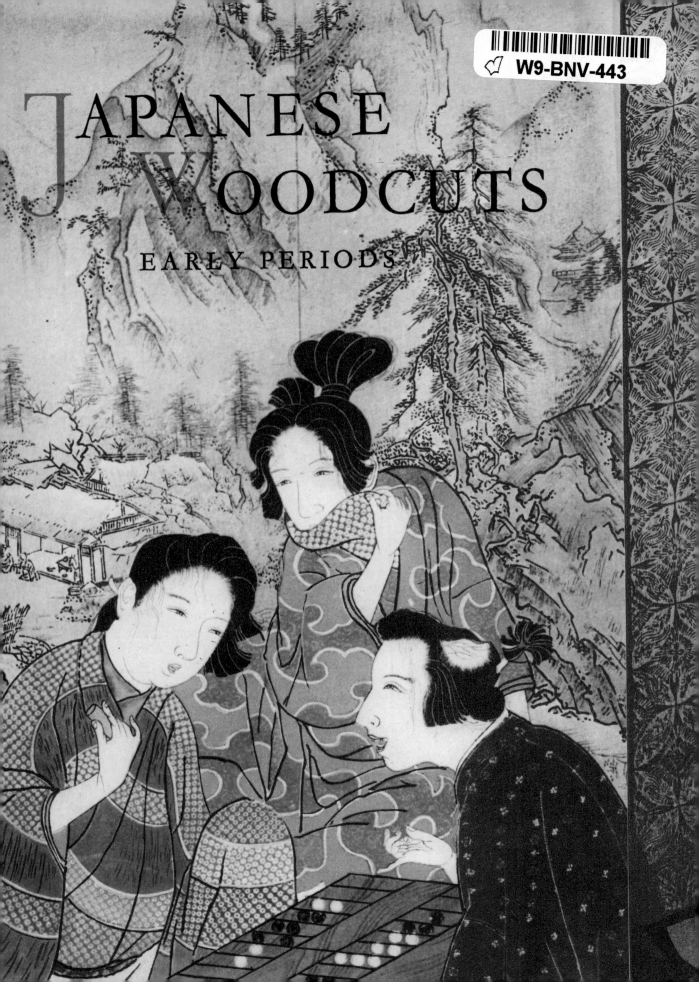

JAPANESE WOODCUTS

EARLY PERIODS

JAPANESE WOODCUTS

HÁJEK - FORMAN

JAPANESE WOODCUTS

EARLY PERIODS

SPRING BOOKS

Translated by Till Gottheiner

Designed and produced by Artia for
SPRING BOOKS
Spring House • Spring Place • London N W 5
Printed in Czechoslovakia
S B 21a - S 602

CONTENTS

LIST OF ILLUSTRATIONS

COLOUR PLATES

INTRODUCTION

The story of Japanese woodcuts has been told many times in Europe. It has not only been the colourful beauty of the Japanese prints which has roused great interest, but also the exciting and illuminating history of their development, and the fact that these woodcuts sensitively recorded the birth of and struggle for artistic expression, improvements in the technique of artistic reproduction, the history of certain towns and the history of all Japan during one of its most interesting phases.

E. F. Strange relates that the first collector of Japanese woodcuts was Isaac Tinsingh, for fourteen years an employee of the Dutch East India Company in Japan, whose legacy (1812) included, among others, several coloured prints *(Japanese Illustrations*, London, 1904, p. XIX). He was almost certainly not the only member of the Dutch East India Company in eighteenth century Nagasaki with an appreciative attitude to this art and to the cultural life of the young bourgeoisie of Edo (today's Tokyo). The representatives of this company are reported to have been in contact with Utamaro, Hokusai and Shiba Kokan, and in 1762 Hirada Gennai, Harunobu's patron and co-worker, sent to his Dutch friend in Nagasaki a book of his poems, *Umi no Sachi*, illustrated with coloured prints.

The effect of these relations between the Japanese painters and the Dutchmen is revealed already in the forties of the eighteenth century on sheets by Masanobu and Shinenaga which have European perspective (uki-e). Rumpf has even tried to detect an European influence on the works of Torii Kiyonobu, who worked at the beginning of the eighteenth century.

European interest in the Japanese woodcuts heightened during the second half of the nineteenth century, when the first examples appeared at exhibitions. Around the turn of the century, a number of large private and public collections grew up both in Europe and America. The artistic quality of the Japanese woodcuts stimulated some Western painters into admiration and imitation. At that time also the main Prague collections were started by Joe Hloucha in the year 1901 and by painter Emil Orlík in 1900–01. The history of the Japanese woodcut became a subject for investigation, and a number of authors tried to relate its story. In France there were E. de Goncourt, Vignier and Inada, followed at a later date by Aubert.

In England there were Satow, W. Anderson, E. F. Strange, later Binyon and O'Brien-Sexton.

In Germany and Austria there were von Seidlitz, Kurth, Succo and Perzyňski.

In America there were E. F. Fenollosa and W. Gookin.

The historical account of the Japanese woodcut gained in precision when the Japanese themselves turned to this subject, setting up exhibitions and initiating the comparative study of preserved reproductions with records of various aspects of their cultural and political history. The results of their studies, published by Shotaro, Shoin, Shibui, Inoue, Noguchi and others, as well as of those gained by the scholarly approach of some modern authors in the West (F. Rumpf, L. W. Ledoux, K. Toda, Sh. Hirano, Hillier), make the story of Japanese prints more and more interesting.

It would, however, be vain to deny that the wave of general interest in Japanese prints is now on the ebb. The tide of our times, which brought a change in taste and a change in artistic appreciation, has swept out of our horizon the great achievements of Japanese woodcutting along with the outlook of that period in the past when the romantic attitude to 'japonaiseries' jubilantly proclaimed the triumph of the woodcut. Only isolated collectors have remained faithful to Japanese woodcuts and few new ones are following in their footsteps. This may be explained also by the fact that the majority of good prints are in permanent collections and the less good ones that appear on the market usually fail to rouse enthusiasm.

Most of the large collections were sold at auctions or privately during the first quarter of this century. This refers to the Paris collections of Hayashi, Gillot, Barboutou, Gonse and Haviland, the German collections of Jaekel, Meyl, Straus-Negbaur and Dankwerts, May and Jackin in London, Ficke and Rouart in America.

Nevertheless, if we manage to overcome certain feelings of sophistication we are forced to admit that the culminating work of the Japanese masters in woodcutting and the entire Japanese art of the woodcut as a phenomenon in itself is and will always remain an acknowledged fact in world history of art. The woodcut will survive all temporary abatements in popularity. Its story will be related and explained again and again, in ways varying according to the time and place, in the same way as the Japanese themselves have for centuries repeated their age-old romances. We shall gain a new understanding of the inter-relation between the economic and political history of Japan and the woodcut, evaluate anew its varying styles and painters, re-examine each individual sheet.

Strangely enough, the majority of older authors have tried to tell the story of Japanese woodcuts in terms of individual masters. In their books the names of schools and painters pass in well-arranged ranks as at a parade, regardless of whether the reader understands the origin, aims and reasons for their work. In interpretations by Japanese authors this march of painters is replaced by a similar parade of names, marking individual eras of the period of Tokugawa. Here the masters of woodcutting are inserted, as it were, into ready-made pigeon-holes. This method of interpretation is a little more graphic since it places the Japanese woodcut in its natural inter-relation with the period and the external factors accompanying its birth and growth.

In defining the period of Japanese woodcuts the authors are all agreed on a division according to the technical methods of printing. The year 1765 is taken as a dividing mark; for at this time sheets with more than five colours began to make their appearance; the period prior to that date is usually called the period of the 'primitives'.

Some time ago L. Bachhofer (*Die Kunst der japanischen Holzschnittmeister*, Munich, 1922) tried to define period in Japanese woodcutting according to developments in style. Basing his work on Wölfflin's teaching and methods he tried to characterize the pre-classical, classical and post-classical eras in Japanese woodcuts. This approach was not entirely successful as it led to the wrong evaluation of individual painters.

The development of Japanese woodcuts was, of course, much more complex than indicated on the Wölfflinian time-scale. The course of events in Japanese society and economy during the seventeenth, eighteenth and nineteenth century was extremely complicated, too, and the woodcut reflected this process with the sensitivity of a seismograph. I am not sure that any time-classification can truthfully depict the main stimulants and trends which led to the development of the Japanese woodcut. Nevertheless, the attempt at a correct historical classification must at the present time be considered a recommendable means for anybody who wants to relate the story of the Japanese woodcut.

In doing so, I will try to employ all the useful and accessible information collected by my predecessors, as well as the material placed at my disposal by Czech japanologists (Prof. Průšek, V. Hilská, J. Neústupný). I am especially indebted to the last-named friend of mine, J. Neústupný, for his deciphering of Japanese inscriptions and for his useful suggestions.

The woodcuts illustrating this book are mostly printed by the kind permission of the National Art Gallery in Prague and the most important of our collectors of Japanese woodcuts, J. Hloucha.

I FROM HOKE-KYO SUTRA TO KOETSU

Development of the Specific Features

This volume is devoted to the earliest period in the development of Japanese woodcuts, from their first appearance to roughly the year 1765 when important changes took place. The term woodcut clearly delimits the technique of artistic reproduction; but we shall take into account in equal measure the style, themes and contents, for each of these had its specific features in the Japanese woodcuts. All four rank equally in importance, even if at different times one or other of them always stood in the fore of the whole development.

The specific features of technique are easily formulated. The question was to reproduce a picture (painted by brush on thin paper) by means of a wooden block. The print was either monochrome (sometimes hand-coloured), or polychrome. In regard to polychrome prints it should be said that in contrast to Chinese coloured prints, in Japan additional blocks printed the coloured areas or ornaments within the outlines printed black by the key block. The Chinese coloured prints use colour in free patches not contoured by black outlines. Consequently, the printing did not require such precision in application. In the Japanese technique, guide-marks (kento) are used, in the way it is done in modern industrial reproduction. These guide-marks are placed in the corners of each block so that the colours register in the correct position (see T. Tukono's article in Smithsonian Report, pp. 221 *seq.*)

The specific features of style are more difficult to indicate. Undeniably, the development of the woodcuts moved within the limitations of the tradition which we call the national style of Japanese painting (yama-to-e). Sometimes the designers of woodcuts are called ukiyo-e painters,

though it is not correct to use this word in connection with any school or style. According to recent research, this expression did not appear until 1682, and even later on it was used only by the public, not by the designers themselves. Moronobu, Sukenobu, Shigenage and others called themselves yamato-e-shi, i. e., followers of the yamato-e style. The woodcut designers made use of some of the principles employed by the classical schools of painting. Then there were still other trends and circumstances that helped to form the specific style of the woodcuts and that did not appear in any other school of painting. To name but a few: the technical scope, the size (a book page or a loose sheet of prescribed dimensions), the connection with textile designs, with the theatre, perhaps even the influence of the folk painting of Otsu (otsu-e) and European painting.

As to the themes particular to woodcuts, most frequently we meet with genre pictures of women and actors. In this respect, it is perhaps correct to use the expression ukiyo-e. This term was taken over from Chinese Buddhist terminology ('fushih', i. e., passing, vanishing world) and in classical literature it conveys the pessimism and vanity of life. Later, this term was used in the sense of 'daily life', 'modern life', etc. In this sense the term was applied to painting and literature in the Tokugawa period. It should, however, not be forgotten that not only the designers of prints, but also many painters of the classical school selected ukiyo themes. On the other hand, genre pictures were not the only themes of woodcuts, for valuable pictures of animals, birds, landscapes, legendary and historical scenes, scenes from novels, and portraits exist in large numbers. It is, therefore, not correct to identify the term ukiyo-e with woodcuts.

The specific content of woodcuts, that is, the specific purpose of the designers of woodcuts, was determined by the customers for whom they were intended: the broad strata of the Japanese bourgeois society. In other words, the aim of the woodcuts differed basically from that of the paintings which were meant mainly for the court and the nobility. They differed from that of the Buddhist pictures as well as from folk art designed for the rural inhabitants. To avoid confusion, let us add that the engraver did not express all interests of his clients; he ignored their economic problems just as he did not include intimate emotional affairs or any aspect of private life. It can be said that the great majority of woodcuts were aimed at satisfying the public interest in various forms of entertainment.

An investigation into the origins of Japanese woodcuts must take into account all these four elements: a specific technique, a specific style, specific themes and specific content. To none of them separately can we ascribe the merit of bringing about that phenomenon, the Japanese woodcut of the Edo period. If, for example, we think of the woodcut purely in terms of a technique of reproduction, its beginnings must be sought as early as in the eighth century. The oldest dated and preserved print from a wooden block is a picture of lions printed on white leather, dated 740. Dated and undated prints have been preserved also from the period between the 8th and 17th centuries (see Rumpf: *Meister des Japanischen Farbenholzschnittes*, p. 4, and *Ryerson Collection* XXXI). Most of them are devoted to Buddhist themes, representing the founders of sects, saints, etc. They were originally cut and printed for the believers in the monasteries, and for generations copied in identical form. Evidence shows that the old samples were copied again and again but only a few new compositions were created, and we are usually at a loss as to how to date them. They added nothing but the rudiments of technical principles for the later development of Japanese woodcuts.

I am, therefore, of the opinion that we should reckon among the forerunners of the Japanese woodcuts in our sense of the word only those works where also others of the elements cited are joined to the technique of woodcutting. In the first place I mean the pictures on fans, which an unknown writer in the middle of the twelfth century used as a background on which he copied the Buddhist text *Hoke-kyo* (Saddharma Pundarika sutra). Originally, there were ten albums of such fans; today only six are preserved, five in the Shitenno-ji Temple in Osaka and one in the National Museum in Tokyo, (compare *National Treasures of Japan*, series I, Catalogue of Art Objects, Registered as National Treasures for the year 1951. Picture catalogue No 7). On the fan-shaped paper background, over which mica and silver and gold dust has been scattered, there are various pictures outlined in black and richly coloured. Originally, it was assumed that this was the Tsukuri technique, currently used for decorative pictures of a similar type: the outlines were first drawn in ink, then covered with a layer of white-wash, coloured, and finally the outlines were retraced. On one of the fans the colour was accidentally washed away and it can be clearly seen that the background was printed with wooden blocks. The themes of these pictures have nothing in common with the Buddhist texts written across the picture. They represent pictures of birds, children, scenes from the well-known romances, and various genre pictures showing the daily life of various classes in Japan at that time, ranging from court life to village environments (see page 22). Not only in regard to the technique and theme, but in regard to style, too, these fans fall into our scheme, for they are typical examples of the yamato-e style. The composition and the setting is created mainly by architectonic elements seen obliquely from above as if through a roof (the Japanese call this 'roofless houses') and through the clouds which extend horizontally along the edges of the pictures. The tectonic elements and the straight lines in which the draperies of the figures are cut form a kaleidoscopic medley of irregular angles. The landscape elements are marked mainly by solitary trees with softly twining branches and flatly stylized foliage, field boundaries and banks, etc. The figures rise out of the geometrical areas of the draperies with head and limb movements of such vigour and energy as to seem almost grotesque. The areas of the faces, limited on one side by black patches of hair, and, on the other, by a simple curve, are indicated in only a few lines, one for the eye, and two meeting at an angle to form the nose (the style called 'hikime-kagihana' by the Japanese). The last question to be answered concerns the content, the aims of these fan pictures. They were carried out in a fairly costly manner to serve as a background for luxury editions of sacred texts, which in the 12th and 13th century were made to order for powerful aristocratic families. Nevertheless, it must be stated that their content was not directed to the interests either of the nobility or the clergy – and the method of reproduction by means of woodcuts is in itself proof of large-scale production. We also know that already at that time large numbers of such fans were exported to China. They must have

22

been objects of current use, so current, in fact, that they seemed hardly worth while preserving unless someone, in an idle moment, used them as background on which to copy a sacred text. They must have been intended for the broader strata of the population, and some sheets at least bear proof that the artist had in mind the simple pleasures and amusements of the people, the environment of mass entertainment and merry-making. Indeed, some of the pictures might have been drawn by Sukenobu, Masanobu or Hokusai. This means that already in the 12th century there existed the first pictures of which we can state, even though with a certain reserve, that the technique used was woodcutting, the style, yamato-e, the subject matter, partly genre, and that they were intended for the entertainment of the broadest sections of the population.

Our reserve concerns mainly the last point, for there seems to have been a certain parallelism rather than connection between the painted fans and the woodcuts of the seventeenth to nineteenth century. The paintings on the fans of the Hoke-kyo Sutra probably formed part of the secular, aristocratic culture and art which arose in the Heian period. They are an expression of the growth of feudal power and feudal society. The woodcuts of the Edo period, on the contrary, formed an integral part of the culture and art of the bourgeoisie, a proof of the growth of the power of the middle classes in Japan.

There seems to be no continuity of development between the woodcuts on the fans with the sutras and the woodcuts of the Edo period, if this development is followed from the aspect of technique. A narrow bridge is formed only by a few legendary biographies of Buddhist patriarchs, a form of literature that seems to have become so popular that the works were not only illustrated in the painted hand-scrolls, but were set with blocks at a later stage, and these woodcut reproductions were distributed all over the country. This, for example, was the case with the book *Yuzumembutsu Engi* that deals with events and stories about the founder of the Nembutsu sect, Ryonin Shonin – a printed copy from the year 1414 is mentioned by Kenji Toda *(Ryerson Collection* p. XXXII) – and the well-known legend of the life of the monk Kukai Kobo Daishi, the founder of the Shingon sect, was illustrated in the fourteenth century by the painter

Tosa Yukimitsu and appeared later as a woodcut. F. Rumpf *(Ise Mono-gatari*, note 23 on page 56) mentions a woodcut edition of a scroll from the year 1593 under the name of *Koya Daishi Gyoki Zuga* and the same in book form in 1596 and 1620. In a similar manner printed editions of some classical romances (e. g., the *Ise Monogatari* and *Genji Monogatari*) form a bridge between woodcuts on fans and the works produced at Edo, as we shall see below.

A direct continuity of the trends shown on the fan pictures can be followed easily in regard to style. It stands beyond doubt that the yamato-e style was brought to life by the secular culture of the later Heian period (12th to 13th century) when it began to appear on the scrolls containing novels, legends and biographies, etc. Some of the outstanding examples of this kind are as follows: 1. The illustrations to the novel by Mrs. Mura-saki Shikibu, the *Genji Monogatari*. This illustrated manuscript was origi-nally a scroll and is now divided into sheets, some of which are in the Reimei-kai Collection in Tokyo, the rest in the Taro Masuda Collection in Kanagawa (compare *National Treasures of Japan*, series II, Catalogue of Objects Registered as National Treasures for the year 1952, picture cata-logue No 17); 2. The illustrations to the legends about Myoren, called *Shigisan Engi*, three scrolls now in the possession of the Chogosonshi-ji Temple in Nara (compare *National Treasures of Japan*, series I, picture cata-logue No 6); 3. The illustrations to the diary of Mrs. Murusaki Shikibu in four scrolls, now in the Masa-uji Collection in Tokyo; 4. The illustra-tions to the history of the burning of the Oten Gate, *Ban Dainagon Eko-toba*, in three scrolls, now in the Tedakatsu Collection in Tokyo; 5. The illustrations to the biography of the statesman Sugawara Michizane, *Kitano Tenjin Engi*. The oldest version (Jokyu) from the year 1219 is preserved in the Kitano Jinja Temple in Kyoto in eight scrolls. The temple library also contains several other versions from later periods (compare Noritake Tsuda: *Handbook of Japanese Art*, Tokyo, 1935, part II, Guide to Temples and Museums, p. 394).

In these pictures of the Heian period the style already shows great variations, ranging from strongly decorative stylization to realistic narra-tive with clever drawings. The 'History of the Shigi-san Temple', and the

'History of Ban Dainagon' contain humorous, even vulgar illustrations; this is even more blatant in the illustrations to 'Various Diseases', *Yamai-no Soshi*, in the Sekido Collection and in the scrolls on 'Humorous Animals', *Choju-giga*, attributed to Toba Sojo (now in the Kozan Monastery in Kyoto). Genre themes appear at that time only in the illustrations to the 'Poets' Meeting at Tohoku' (now in the National Museum in Tokyo), where situations from the lives of people of the most varied social standing are depicted.

The painters of later centuries inherited the yamato-e style together with the themes taken from legends and novels used for these first paintings. The apex was reached in the sixteenth and seventeenth century when the painters of the Tosa and Kano schools adapted both the themes and style of the early yamato-e. In the scrolls by Tosa Mitsunobu (1434 and 1525) the yamato-e style is found almost in the form that was later taken over by woodcuts, i. e., the drawing was carried out with a strong calligraphic line and the landscape elements resemble the Chinese style of ink drawings. The line laid down by Mitsunobu was followed by Tosa Mitsumochi, Tosa Mitsushige, and Sumiyoshi Jokei, and that of the Kano school mainly by Sanraku. But ultimately the school of Koetsu and Sotatsu considered itself the legitimate heir to the yamato-e tradition; it was represented by the works of Honnami Koetsu (1568–1637), Tawaraya Sotatsu (about 1615–1635), his son Sosetsu, Ogata Korin (1658–1716) and his brother Kenzan. This outstanding group of artists was of wide cultural significance for the period. Their activities did not begin and end with painting and poetry, but embraced sword-making, ceramics, lacquering and even the production of paper. Sometimes they are spoken of as representatives of the culture of the new rich bourgeoisie (Korin, indeed, was the son of a rich business man), but this is not correct. Their art was exclusively the art of the aristocracy, one might say the art of the over-cultivated aristocracy, and most of their work was intended for the nobility. It is of interest to examine what happened to the yamato-e style in their hands. Its decorative elements were emphasized till they reached an almost contra-realistic conception. The subject matter was simplified and re-cast in the rhythmic play of forms, lines and colours, on the exciting map of hitherto uncharted continents. These are the most perfect of lines, the most perfect of shapes and the most perfect of colours, moving the spectator almost to cry out with sheer sensual pleasure. But they are lines, shapes and colours with but a hair's breadth of connection with the subject matter, leading into a sphere bordering on formalism. They could go no further. And, in fact, the yamato-e style of this variation found no continuation in Japan and the remarkable works by Sotatsu and Korin did not find any followers.

Nevertheless, we should pause to look at three pictures by Korin, where the decorativeness is perhaps less orgiastic than in his other works. These are the picture 'Thirty-six Poets' and the two pictures illustrating the story of the *Ise Monogatari* (compare *Ausstellung Altjapanischer Kunst*, Berlin 1939, catalogue 109, and Minamoto, op. cit., No 175). F. Rumpf has pointed out that these compositions were adapted from the pattern by Koetsu – who was his great-uncle – and he used this fact as one of the arguments to support the tradition which makes Koetsu the author of the woodcut designs to the *Ise Monogatari*, published in 1608. If that is the case, then we can say that the autochthonic development of the yamato-e school not only ended in the Koetsu school, but also found in this school possibilities for a new life in the woodcut prints of the Edo period.

Prior to the first popular books illustrated with woodcuts one more event occurred which certainly must have influenced the first woodcut illustrations. These were the so-called Nara-bon books, published in the fifteenth and sixteenth century. They were hand-written, and hand-illustrated, did not have the form of scrolls but of bound books, and were clearly produced in large numbers as popular literature. On the whole, they spread classical secular and semi-secular literature which thus gained a wide audience. For example, the collection of the Ryerson Library in Chicago contains one of the Nara books that relates the story of *Taisho-kan* ('On the Ancestors of the Fujiwara Family'), the story of General Minamoto-no Mitsunaga *(Manju)*, the story of *Utsubo Monogatari* and *Soga Monogatari* and others (see *Ryerson Collection* p. 5–13). Similarly, the illustrated book of classical poems in the collection of the Prague National Gallery belongs among this group of popular literature and is a direct antecedent of the printed books of the seventeenth century (see plate 6). A similar book of poems with fan illustrations was one of the first printed books with woodcuts to appear after 1600 under the name of Ogi-no Soshi by Koetsu. (K. Wade reprinted this book in 1917 in Tokyo). The style of the illustrations in all these Nara books is a direct descendant of the yamato-e scrolls, but as a popular version pays more attention to a brief account of facts than to ostentatious decorativeness. This rustification of the yamato-e tradition in the Nara-bon books was probably a decisive factor in the formation of the style of the 17th century woodcut illustrations and I wonder that Rumpf overlooked this circumstance in his penetrating study of this topic *(Das Ise Monogatari von 1608)*.

In summing up we might say that the time between the twelfth and sixteenth century was a preparatory period for the Japanese woodcut. This was the time during which its specific technique and its specific style gradually evolved. The first indications of the specific theme and aims of woodcuts began to appear, not to mature, however, in the following period.

II FROM ISE MONOGATARI TO KYO WARABE

The Grouping of Specific Features

Rumpf expressed the categorical opinion that the originator of the Japanese woodcuts was the illustrator of the printed edition of the *Ise Monogatari* published in the year 1608. In his excellent thesis dated 1931 Rumpf reached the conclusion that Honami Koetsu (1586–1637) was very likely the designer of the illustrations, and further that his designs influenced the woodcut illustrations of the entire seventeenth century in a very definite manner.

This book of the *Ise Monogatari* was published in Kyoto in 1608 in two volumes containing 49 illustrations. It was printed in Japanese lettering designed by Koetsu on multicoloured chalk paper that might also have been produced in Koetsu's workshop. The publisher was Suminokura Soan, one of Koetsu's pupils, a well-known poet, calligrapher, painter, genealogist, and patron of the arts, son of a rich shipbuilder.

This luxury edition was obviously intended for court circles. But in the same year a popular edition appeared in smaller size; and two years later a third edition; later the book went through a number of further editions. All contained the same illustrations with only slight changes until the sixties of the seventeenth century. Though some authors have tried to indicate that the technique of cutting and printing is primitive and rough, this is not really the case. The woodcuts of the first edition were probably cut by Shimomura Tukifusa; the popular editions were printed from blocks which were cut by him in a slightly smaller format with such precision that at first sight the impression is gained that both editions were printed from identical blocks.

The style of these illustrations is largely characteristic of the yamato-e tradition. On comparing them with the yamato-e pictures of the Heian and Kamakura periods we see that they are not so decoratively stylized into geometrical patterns as, for example, the scrolls of the *Genji Monogatari*, and that the narrative character and the elasticity of lines is closer to the scrolls of the *Shigisan Engi* or *Kitano Tenjin Engi*. As to later works in the yamato-e tradition, they are primarily reminiscent of the pictures by Tosa Mitsunobu and Tosa Mitsumochi – and I think Rumpf is wrong in denying this connection with the Tosa school. There is evidence, too, of its connection with the rusticized yamato-e of the Nara books. In both cases the architectonic elements are often replaced by landscape themes, which are similarly stylized in the Chinese tradition. The same proportion of the size of the figures to the environment can be detected. The stylization of clouds, which cover the upper and lower edges in horizontal shaded puffs, resembles the yamato-e pictures of the period around 1600 (Tosa Mitsuyoshi and Kano Sanraku). The figures, too, are drawn in thin lines on the ceremoniously arranged garments and have faces of the hikime-kagihana type.

In regard to themes, the *Ise Monogatari* of the year 1608 presents the first woodcuts in a book with secular contents. But the subject matter is neither the genre type nor contemporary, but a traditional collection of 125 anecdotes from the life of the poet Ariwara Narihira, a Japanese version of the Don Juan theme, composed approximately in the twelfth century. It was considered to be literature for women, and the author of the epilogue to the woodcut edition of 1608, Yasokuso, dedicated this edition, too, to the women. In other words, it had a secular theme in the sense that culture and art of the Heian and Kamakura periods were secular.

The pictures depict intimate forms of entertainment which arose as a part of the aristocratic Heian-Kamakura culture and which in the 17th century were becoming popular among the broader strata of the Japanese population. The pictures were probably intended for court circles and for the nobility, as well as for leading groups of the bourgeoisie whose economic power was on the increase.

It seems that the popularization, possibly rustification, of aristocratic art and culture was a characteristic trend in Japanese culture during the

sixteenth and seventeenth century; popularization seems also to have been the aim of the first Japanese printed books with woodcuts. This trend was greatly aided by the expansion of the printing workshops. Until the end of the sixteenth century the only printing works existing in Japan were those of the monasteries. After Hideyoshi's two expeditions to Korea in 1592 and 1597, many Chinese and Korean books were brought back and even whole sets of printing types which were part of the great loot of the war. This enabled noble families and even private individuals to set up printing houses. In Kyoto there were about five private printing firms which published popular editions of classical novels, legends and heroic stories, called Kana-zoshi ('books printed in kana letters'). They were intended for the broad section of the population that did not know the complicated system of Chinese writing. The most popular of these Kana-zoshi books were those published by Koetsu (called Koetsu-bon) and his pupil Soan (called Saga-bon after his place of residence). One of the new printing houses to be founded at this time was the Jesuit printing house in Amakusa which published books in Japanese printed in the Latin alphabet. One of the first books to be translated into Japanese was 'Aesop's Fables' *(Esopo no Fabulas)* published in Amakusa in 1593.

From about 1625 on, the woodcuts in books were hand-coloured with vermilion red (tan) and green made from copper oxide (rokushu). These two colours gave the books their name 'Tan-roku-bon'. Later blue was added, then yellow, ochre and mauve, and books with these hand-coloured illustrations were given the name edori-bon – 'coloured little books'.

Since the bourgeois part of the population, who purchased these first books with woodcuts, had mostly a passive share in the culture of the country at the beginning of the seventeenth century, we can assume that at the time they were still not very powerful. The social structure and state organisation, introduced by the three unifiers of the country (Nabunaga, Gideyoshi, Iyeyasu), were still strong enough at first, and the privileged classes of noblemen and soldiers held all the powerful positions in the state until the suppression of the Shimabar rebellion (1637). Only after this date did they probably begin to lose their *raison d'être*. We know that only by the middle of the seventeenth century was the system of wage labour beginning to oust the slave system and the towns began to grow in size and importance. In 1625, Kyoto had 240,000 inhabitants, Osaka possibly 280,000, and Edo only 150,000 (compare Yosaburo Takekoshi, *The Economic Aspects of the History of the Civilisation of Japan*, London, 1930, vol. II, pp. 57–59, 245, 257).

Nevertheless, the woodcut, as a matter of interest in bourgeois Japanese culture, the woodcut as a phenomenon in itself, was already in existence, not only in the form of the illustrated romances of the *Ise Monogatari*, but also in dozens of other Kana-zoshi, Tan-roku-bon and Edori-bon editions. A book that went through many editions was the popular biography of Nichiren, called '*Nichiren-shonin Chu-ga-san*', published for the first time with woodcuts in 1632 (see *Ryerson Collection*, p. 26). Other typical literature of the time includes the epos on the lives of military leaders and heroes, some of which were recited by blind bards. The *Catalogue of the Ryerson Collection* included stories from the life of Minamoto no Yoshitsune, '*Gikei ki*', published in 1635 and 1659, *Hogen Monogatari* and *Heiji Monogatari* from the year 1657 and others.

But in adhering to our classification according to these four aspects of technique, style, theme and contents, we discover that it still did not possess what we called the specific theme of woodcuts, the genre subject. According to popular tradition, the inventor of the Japanese genre picture was the painter Iwasa Matabei, who was hence considered the forefather of the woodcut prints. The majority of scholars, however, have expressed doubts about this theory. Iwasa Matabei (1578–1650), also called Shoi or Doun, was the son of a nobleman, Araki Murashige; he studied painting under Kano Shoei and Tosa Mitsunori. He called himself a member of the Tosa school on some of his paintings. An unconfirmed report relates that the people called him Ukiyo Matabei, i. e., Matabei of the Passing World, and that he was the founder od the actual ukiyo-e school. An exhibition in 1929, during which all his work was collected in the National Museum in Tokyo, did not prove him to have been in direct contact with the genre ukiyo-e paintings. Pictures signed by him (self-portraits, portraits of 36 poets, and screens with episodes from the *Ise Monogatari*) seem to have little in common with that style; on the contrary, his authorship is not vouched for in regard to pictures with a genre topic and ascribed to him. So it would seem that his work was 'far from that realism which is the vital substance of the popular school describing the life and manners of life of the lower classes' as Yone Noguchi aptly wrote (*The Ukiyo-e Primitives*, p. 6).

But even if we leave Iwasa Matabei aside, the development of the genre theme can be clearly followed from the end of the sixteenth century on. Interest turned first to outdoor scenes, excursions, merry-making and so on (see plates 4 and 5). The best-known pictures of this kind include the picture 'An Outing' shown in the Shinden Hall of the Emman-in monastery at Otsu, the screen 'An Autumn Excursion to the Tako Mountain' by Kano Hideyori, now in the Fukuoka Collection, 'The Festival at the Hokoku-jinja Temple' by Kano Naizena, the screen with the picture of artisans by Kano Yoshinobu, and 'The Blossom Feast' by Kano Naganobu. It would seem that the genre themes increased in popularity throughout the first half of the seventeenth century. Around the fifties interest began to turn away from the outdoor scenes to interiors, to pictures of dancers and musicians, of women and men at leisure. The crowd scenes gave way to figures of individual persons who stood in the foreground. The depiction of landscapes with architectural features was replaced by elaborately drawn draperies. Pictures of this kind exist in large numbers (mostly on screens). Unfortunately, however, most of them have remained anonymous and can be dated only with great difficulty. The best-known is the Hikone screen with the pictures of four types of entertainments, now in the Naitada Ii Collection in Tokyo (see plates 7–11 showing a later woodcut replica of this outstanding painting). It used, wrongly, to be ascribed to Matabei. Another is the screen with six dancing girls in the Kyoto Museum, which at the Exhibition of Japanese Art in Berlin was wrongly dated in the period around 1600. Probably it is half a century younger (see *Ausstellung Altjapanischer Kunst*, Berlin 1939, No 121). Yone Noguchi reproduces some outstanding anonymous pictures from the Matabei Exhibition in Tokyo: 'A Game of Cards', and the screen with 'The Festive Dance of Summer'. A number of such typical

pictures can also be found in European collections (see *Collection Gillot, Objets d'art et peintures d'Extrême Orient*, Paris 1902, vol. I., 2076–2081).

Rumpf, in following the development of illustrations in the *Ise Monogatari*, reached the conclusion that certain important changes in style took place about 1660. Instead of outlines and folds cut in straight lines the forms became more compact and the lines fluid. The designs of the draperies showed elaborate decorative motifs as introduced by the fashion in design called Bingata from the island of Ryukyu. Landscapes, too, became more decorative, less crowded and less hastily drawn. These changes in style are even more noticeable in other books with woodcuts published around 1660, particularly so in the short story 'The Clan of Miura' (*Miura Monogatari*, 1657), and in the collection 'Rules of Etiquette for Ladies' (*Onna Shorei Shu*, 1660). The composition began to be adapted to the shape of a book page and the larger figures were placed into more prominent positions, framed by landscape or architectonic elements. The placing of the black accents of the print began to acquire harmonious rhythm. The border of clouds, which previously had covered a considerable part of the pictures from top to bottom, was pushed to the edges or vanished altogether. Both the contours of the draperies and the profile of the heads became more fluent, with faces that gained in expression and details. The specific features of the woodcut style attained their maturity; the picture is no more a copy of the yamato-e scrolls, but an autochthonous composition, designed as a book page.

On seeking some genre topic in these books from about 1660 or at least some topical themes, we have to look at the pioneering work in the publication, 'The Kyoto Boys' *(Kyo Warabe)*, which deals with the sights of Kyoto and its surroundings. The author was Nagawara Kiun, the publisher Yamamori Rukubei, who put it on the market in 1658 with 82 illustrations by an anonymous painter (see *Ryerson Collection*, p. 41., plate I). In style the illustrations are reminiscent of the above-cited books; since, however, most of the motifs were outdoor scenes the influence of Chinese landscape painting (or, to be more concrete, that of the Kano school) towards the creation of this specific style in woodcutting is more pronounced. The topical genre themes appeared clearly on some sheets in the fifth volume ('Villagers from Ohara', 'The Sanno Festival at Hiyoshi', 'Fishing on Lake Biwa').

About 1660, then, the Japanese woodcuts developed a specific style of their own and began to use topical themes. Numerous popular illustrated publications appeared on the market at that time. These signs reveal that the transition to an important period in the development of Japanese woodcuts was close at hand.

III MORONOBU AND THE GENROKU PERIOD

Integration of Specific Features

The various elements of Japanese woodcuts could be found in isolation already in the period prior to 1660. In that year they reached organic and lasting integration. This integration is connected with the name of the painter Hishikawa Moronobu and with the town of Edo (today's Tokyo). Edo and Moronobu certainly played a great part; nevertheless, they represent no more than the culmination of the preceding development that attained embodiment in a particular artist and place.

Books published prior to 1659 appeared mostly in Kyoto and Osaka; after that year some publishers probably became established in Edo. One of the first illustrated books printed in Edo was the short story, 'Cave on Mount Fuji' *(Ye-iri Fuji no Hito-ana)*, published by Matsuya in 1659 (see *Ryerson Collection*, p. 43). Edo began to forge ahead in woodcut illustrations even though the Kyoto illustrations, too, registered progress in the second half of the seventeenth century, due chiefly to the talent of the painters Hinaya Ryuho and Yoshida Hanbei.

Hinaya Ryuho contributed greatly to illustration as early as 1660, as seen from the book about the young prince Genji *(Osana Genji)* published in 1661. Yoshida Hanbei worked in the period from 1670 to 1700 and according to Rumpf was as important to woodcutting in Kyoto as Moronobu in the Edo woodcuts. Kyoto with its 400,000 inhabitants was still the largest town in the country in 1671; Edo at that time was approaching the 350,000 mark (1673) and its expansion must have been rapid, for this figure represents double the 1625 population. It was becoming the centre not only of the nobility and their vassals and thousands of warriors, but also of the merchants and artisans, leading artists and bold thinkers, such as Yamanaga Sako and Kumezawa Banzan. Edo, far from the cultural sphere of Kamigata (i. e., the area of Kyoto and Osaka), was passing through its heroic period, its pioneering days, a time that lacked all conventions, when gangs of citizens and warriors (Otokodate and Machiyakko) boldly ruled the life and tastes of the city with their sabres.

Hishikawa Moronobu, who originally came from the Awa province to settle in Edo as a textile designer and embroiderer, began his artistic career with illustrations for books published in Kyoto. His first work from the period 1650–1660 did not differ in any way from the older Kyoto illustrations. Yone Noguchi is of the opinion that Moronobu reached maturity as late as in his middle thirties, and that his best work fell into the Kambun period (1661–1672). At that time he began to publish loose sheets as well as book illustrations.

In so far as Moronobu's development can be followed, thanks chiefly to K. Shibui's research (see *Catalogue des Estampes Érotiques*, Tokyo, 1926, which has a large number of Moronobu's titles and very good reproductions), Noguchi is right. His opinion, of course, applies mainly to the work towards the end of the Kambun period, as, for instance, *Makura Byobu* (1669) and *Koshaku Kyara Muraka* (1670). This work must truly be labelled an event of outstanding importance in the history of the Japanese woodcut. A contemporary subject, the men and women of his time, is selected here as the centre of artistic interest. They are not placed in the framework of a picture, but they create the picture, in groups of two or more figures varying in size to take up as much as half the area of the illustration. The environment, architectonic or landscape elements are given as much attention by the painter at this stage as the figures, sometimes more, sometimes perhaps less. By enlarging the figures and placing them in the foreground a feature appeared that was long to accompany the Japanese woodcut through the course of its development, namely, the background which gives the impression of pressing on the figure as in a landscape seen through a telescope.

Around this period the specific style and theme of woodcuts matured in Moronobu's work. The tradition of Japanese illustrations merged with the Chinese tradition of ink painting, or, to be more precise, a break took place with all classical and traditional styles. Of the yamato-e style remained only the composition, which gives a perspective seen obliquely from above. The yamato-e trend towards geometrical design in setting and figure left its heritage in unfortunate compositions ruled mostly by horizontal and vertical lines. The draperies, once angular, found replacement in flowing lines, but they did not yet reach that orgy of curves which was typical of the later development. Some of the angular features of the yamato-e figures left a faint echo in the sharp angle formed at the shoulder. The simplified types of the hikime-kagihana faces are recalled only in the hooked noses of the women. The eyes were sometimes still drawn in simple wavy lines, but most of them are already half-open.

The specific technique of woodcutting showed considerable progress from the point of view of the craft. Few places reveal hard breaks where lines met at angles instead of curves. The print is clear, the soft black colour is spread evenly on large patches. The colouring, however, where used, was indefinite. The person who carried out this function did so with little knowledge and applied the colour merely as red, yellow or green spots and ornaments.

All that remains to be done now is to consider the content and intentions of these prints by Moronobu. This is a more complex task in view of the restricted number of works that have come down to us. It seems that life in the town, the life of the city beaux and belles of the Yoshiwara district began, in the minds and interests of the people, to acquire more significance than the life at the Shogun or the Emperor's court; it outdid in significance even the legends of the heroes and the founders of noble families. The aim of the artist's work was to express this fact for the first time, and to do so with courage and sincerity. Moronobu, of course, was not yet a painter to glorify town life, and if the belles in his pictures are larger than the princes had been in the illustrations of the previous decade, this can be simply explained by the general trends in figure painting. The life and interests of the towns were boldly described here with no small degree of amazement, somewhat clumsy curiosity and no little ardour of novelty.

Moronobu's style, as it evolved around 1670, remained current for almost a quarter of a century without any considerable changes. Only the

41

42

figures became a little larger still after 1680, the lines acquired more gradations and movement and the eyes on the faces gradually became more wide open. It was not until 1690 that this style reached the form which was to become the starting point for further development and which is incorrectly ascribed to Moronobu as his personal contribution. By this we mean those compositions where a small number of figures take up almost the entire area of the picture, where two or more bodies are joined into one area linked by a wild play of curves, and where the background and environment is sometimes reduced to a few essentials. The lines of the contours and folds of the draperies have more exquisitely graceful movements and gradations, and their accents compete with the large ornaments on the kimonos in making the composition a highly sophisticated rhythm. The contents of these perfect black and white prints speak of self-conscious wealth, vain beauty and gross sensuality.

Sheets of this type appeared only towards the close of Moronobu's work, e. g., in the book *Koshoku Goreiko*, published in 1695, and in some albums whose dates are unknown. I think that the emancipation of the figure from its dependence on the background and environment was carried out by Sughimura Jihei, who also enlarged them to full size in the picture and stylized them into a wild rhythm of black lines and patches. This conception was followed by Hishikawa Moroshige and later, after 1700, also by Torii Kiyonobu and Okumura Masanobu (see Shibui, *Estampes Érotiques*, pl. I–XV). The best picture of this group is, in my opinion, the coloured sheet 'Three Heads', on which Kiyonobu formed the bodies of two seated girls and one man into a compact massif, a mountain of lines and colours crowned by three agreeable faces (see Noguchi, *Ukiyo-e Primitives*, pl. 30). The gently harmonized composition of this type was made by Kiyonobu in the first decade of the eighteenth century. They seem to stand in sharp contrast to the brutal robustness of his older sheets and to the robustness of his sheets with actors, which he painted at the same time. One is almost tempted to ascribe those cultivated works to Masanobu and accuse Kiyonobu of publishing another man's work under his own name. Masanobu's pictures of women and lovers are, indeed, indistinguishable from Kiyonobu's pictures from the first decade of the century, as Noguchi has pointed out; but it seems that Masanobu preferred more lively compositions which followed on Moronobu's older work.

The themes of this noteworthy group of woodcuts, which was discussed in the preceding paragraphs, centred around the erotic aspects of life in Edo in the years 1690–1710. Yoshiwara, the quarter of love, which had been reconstructed after the fire in the city in 1657, was undoubtedly one of the most popular urban subjects. Noblemen of the highest rank (Date Masamune of Sendai, Asano Harunaga of Hiroshima, Sakakibara of Echigo and even the lord of Tatebayashi, before he became Shogun Tsunayoshi) came to seek the favours of Takao, one of the renowned belles, and they were closely rivalled by business magnates, whose wealth was mounting into the millions (Kinokunia Bunzaemon, Naraya Mozaemon). The social life of the city was centred around that district, money was flowing lavishly and great rivalry existed in matters of luxurious robes and costly entertainments as we see not only in the woodcuts that relate the gallant life of Yoshiwara at the time of Genroku, but also in the painted pictures (see, e. g., plates 12–14), popular songs and literature of the period.

Only one place rivalled Yoshiwara in popularity. That was Sakae-cho where the theatre world was concentrated. Most of the theatres were of the Kabuki type, which grew up at the beginning of the seventeenth century out of mimes and which in the Genroku period reached a high standard thanks to a number of outstanding actors such as Ichikawa Danjuro, Nakamura Shichisaburo and Nakamura Denkuro. Kabuki was becoming so popular at the time that the serious guardians of public morals were filing complaints: 'The daughters of the samurai, merchants and craftsmen know all about the names and ages of the actors but are ignorant as to who hold the highest offices of the Shogunate. They learn to sing, dance and act instead of learning to sew . . .'

Moronobu was probably the first to take up the popular subject of actors because sheets of his from the years 1675 and 1681 are known on which he depicted the theatre; later this became the almost exclusive monopoly of Torii Kiyonobu. He was already at work in the Genroku period, producing a number of portraits of actors and publishing several

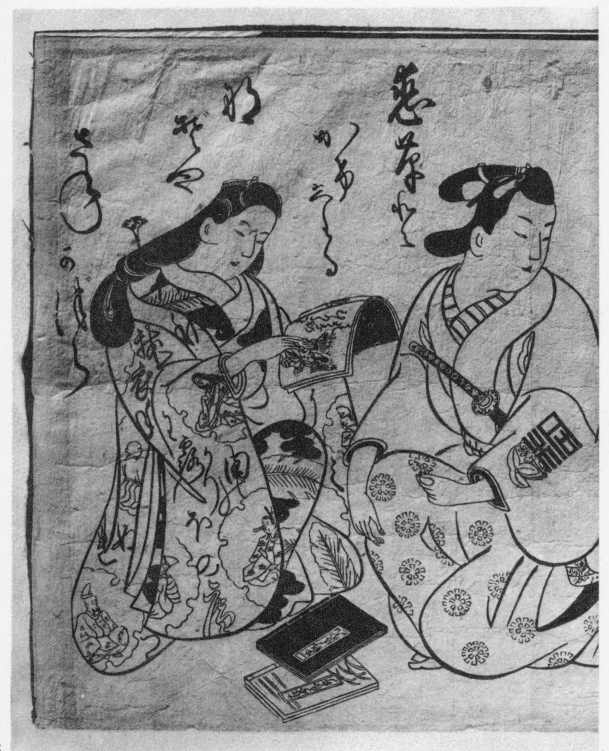

46

books about actors and the theatre. His is the major share in creating and determining the development of this genre of painting. If, however, we were to seek here the picture which in maturity could be compared with contemporary pictures of women and lovers, our search would be vain. Until 1710 the sheets were, in fact, only primitive in revealing the identity of actors and rôles in rough stylizations and empty compositions.

For the Genroku period and the years that followed, i. e., for the two decades from 1690 to 1710, we have to state that maturity was reached only in erotic sheets and pictures of women of the type first introduced by Moronobu in about 1670. Pictures from the theatrical environment and other themes (from the workshops, from rural environments, street scenes, illustrations to contemporary novels and stories) were only beginning to appear. For example, the collection of pictures of various employments, *Wakoku Shoshoku E-zukushi*, by Moronobu, was published in 1685 and the pictures of women at various jobs, *Wakoku Hyaku-jo*, came out in 1695. Contemporary love stories were illustrated by Kiyomasu in 1696 and stories about the actor Shikisaburo by Masanobu in 1708. It is nevertheless remarkable that popular editions of classical novels and poetry were in the Genroku period still numerically in the majority. Not even the style was changed much, but the enlarging of the figure and the freeing of the picture from an elaborate background, introduced about 1670, continued automatically. In contents, the interests of the city population were expressed with increasing self-consciousness. The technique did not show any basic changes in the Genroku period, either.

In fact, changes in technique, form and contents, which mark the beginning of a new epoch in the development of the woodcut, began only after the Genroku period, around 1710. This is not surprising if one realizes that this ran parallel to changes in the social and economic life, in the life in Edo and other towns. Much has been written about the luxury, wealth, immorality and treasures of the merchants in the Genroku period because this state of affairs was still quite exceptional. The same applies to the decline of the power of the samurai. 'Nevertheless, at that time the upper classes and the military rulers were still fighting hard against the power of money and were holding their own against the merchants,' as

Takekoshi informs us (op. cit., p. 355). At that time the wealth of the Osaka family of Yodaya was confiscated without any explanations or grounds, and the noblemen managed to destroy many of the merchants by refusing the return of property they took from them on forced loans. Not only by law, but also in effect the city strata of merchants and craftsmen were still subordinate to the samurai in every respect.

IV FOUR SCHOOLS OF WOODCUTTING

Glorification of the Town

The changes in the social and economic life of Japan are clearly visible on the pictures of the Kyoho period (1715–1733). The progress in industrial and agricultural production was reflected in the increasing home trade while exports went down. The home production of silk, cotton, iron and food made the country less dependent on foreign trade. The general standard of living was going up, the wealth of the country rose considerably, but it was not divided in such a manner as the Shogunate would have wished. The greatest part streamed into the pockets of the merchants, industrialists and farmers, no longer to the nobility and the samurai. Their incomes, dependent on the price of rice, had fallen by one half by 1735, which was partly caused by a monetary reform in the era of Shotoku (1711–1715). 'The history of Japan after 1700 is a record of how the military caste renounced its position to the power of money,' Takekoshi says. In a letter to the Shogun Yoshimune the writer complains that at that time the social position of the samurai was critically declining and that it was becoming impossible to distinguish the samurai from the merchants. The latter, in full confidence that their power was based on the close organization of society and the guilds, did not hesitate to take over the samurai's property, bought their offices and titles or gained them by employing bribery.

Life at Edo was undergoing great changes. The town, which during the Genroku period had consisted mainly of houses with thatched roofs, was beginning to build tiled roofs in the Kyoho period. Gold embroidered silk dresses and brocades, which had previously been a sign of great luxury, were becoming the daily dress of the wives of the samurai

51

and the burghers. The palanquins of the citizens of the lower classes were becoming so much of a common sight that in 1726 the Shogunate had officially to permit their use. Unfortunately, unbridled debauchery, immorality and prostitution were equally common features of city life. 'The girls from Yoshiwara,' Noguchi complains, 'who in the Genroku times were behaving like court ladies are now becoming vulgar prostitutes.' The town was moving from the pioneering rapacity of growth to a wallowing in the spoils.

We devoted more attention to the life of Japan and Edo in the first decades of the eighteenth century in order to discover the character of the changes which at that time affected the development of woodcutting. I think that changes took place primarily in the content, and the causes for this have to be sought in the economic and social life. In short, the Japanese woodcuts changed around 1710 from describing the life and interests of the inhabitants in Edo to a glorification of the town and city entertainments. The belles of Yoshiwara and the actors were no longer merely one of many possible themes of life, but became *the* most popular theme. In regard to style, this fact found expression in a change in the traditional perspective obliquely from above; now for the first time this was replaced (in pictures of women and actors) by a view obliquely from below. The single figure of an actor or a woman which now grew in dimensions to occupy the entire picture, rose in front of the spectator with the monumentality of a giant statue looking down on him from above, menacing him with its size and magnificence. One might speak of deification, for such treatment was otherwise given in the history of Japanese painting only to Buddhist gods. The monumentality of the composition was emphasised by the flow of lines which rise in powerful crests of breaking waves and boldly form strong accents. Finally, the technique was adapted to these changes. At first vermilion red was added in hand-painted areas to strengthen the effect of the thick black lines, and later other colours. Around 1715 urushi appeared, a layer of varnish which gave brilliance to some colours and was added by hand to give the appearance of lacquer.

About 1720 the ornateness of these hand-coloured prints was increased by the application of gold dust.

54

Three persons shared the introducton of these requisites of style and technique in the pictures of this period: Torii I Kiyonobu, Okumura Masanobu and Kaigetsudo Ando. Let us briefly consider the share contributed by each of them.

Kaigetsudo Yasunori Ando (civic name Okasawa Genkichi) and his disciples Dohan, Doshin and Anchi specialized in pictures of 'monumental' female figures, most of whom they painted and only a few of which were designed for woodcuts (see the sets published by Ledoux and Noguchi). The problem of these painters is somewhat complicated by the fact that we do not know when these artists lived. Various sources give these dates for the period of their activities: 1615–1623, 1661–1670, 1704–1715, 1715–1735. Rumpf is of the opinion, based on iconographic evidence, that the most correct date is 1661–1670 (see Meister, p. 141). But from a point of view of style this is quite out of the question and the most likely estimation is Noguchi's, who gives the dates for the Kaigetsudo school as between 1711–1716. Also a quotation from the contemporary author, Yanagisawa Rikyo, 1706–1758, (given by Kenji Tadou, *Ryerson Collection*, p. 129), places Kaigetsudo in the ranks of the painters Hanabusa Itcho, Okumara Masanobu, Torii Kiyonobu, Hanegawa Chincho and Nishikawa Sukenobu.

The search for the inventor of the monumental figure leads most probably to Kiyonobu, whose work is of older origin and who applied his principle of perspective from below not only to pictures of women but also to actors. His is so far the oldest example of a picture in which the whole area is given over to one figure. He left the well-known album of courtesans, *Keisei Ehon*, which appeared in 1700, where some of the standing figures act as a premonition of the 'monumental conception'. The only complete copy of this album is in Chicago (*Ryerson Collection*, p. 116, plate I and III).

But it should be said that the same album appeared in the following year with small changes under the name of Okumura Masanobu, who was in Rumpf's opinion fifteen years older than Kiyonobu and therefore probably did not copy the work of a junior.

Nevertheless the entire conservative character of Masanobu's work

57

prohibits us from suspecting him of having a share in inventing the bombastic style of the early eighteenth century. Perhaps not even the technical aspect of the invention, often ascribed to him, was his work, but rather that of his enterprising son, Okumura Genroku Masanobu.

A very reasonable point of view on this question was expressed by Noguchi, who writes: 'Instead of seeking to know whether Kaigetsudo influenced Kiyonobu or vice versa, it would be more correct to say by way of answer that both flourished side by side in the spirit of the time.' Expressed in figures, the period of the great flourishing of the monumental style lay probably between 1710 and 1725.

At that time the best works came out of the workshops of Torii; sheets endowed with a passionate energy and erudition, as, for example, the picture of the actor Nakajima Kanzaemon in the wild role of Royaburi Kagekiyo (see Kurth, *Masterpieces of Japanese Woodcuts*, Berlin, 1924, pl. 3), 'Heikuro and Heikichi', 'Danjuro in Shibaraku', and also the votive tablets of Goro and Asahino in the Kwanon Temple in Nako, 'The Struggle of Watanabe no Tsuna with the Demon' and 'The Fight of Shoki with the Imp' *(Catalogue of the Tony Straus-Negbaur Collection*, Berlin, 1928, No 16, 17). The list of his monumental pictures of geishas and actors in female roles should include chiefly 'The Woman with Flowers' in the National Museum in Tokyo, two sheets from the Matsukata collection (Noguchi, pl. 29–45) and the sheet with actor Nakamura Senya from the Straus-Negbaur Collection (13) and others. In our collection this phase of development is represented only by the sheet of actor Tsugawa Kamon in a female part (plate 17). Outstanding pictures by other painters include 'The Courtesan Kokonoie' by Hanegawa Chincho and the composition of 'Courtesans from Three Towns' by Masanobu (see Noguchi, op. cit., pl. 22, 53).

The grandiose conception of these pictures and the fervour of their drawing makes them one of the most attractive groups in the collection of Japanese woodcuts. 'One feels, however, that such pictures can pass muster only as a passing experiment,' Noguchi, with rare perception, observed. For, fortunately, the period which is characterized by its bombastic and exaggeratedly self-conscious creation, was comparatively short in the

59

history of each culture. The monumental conception was continued in Japanese woodcuts for a further ten to fifteen years in a moderate and largely schematic form. It is apparent mainly in the numerous works that arose in Torii's workshop (where after 1725 the leading master was Kiyonobu II), in the workshop of Okumura (Toshinobu and Okumura Genroku, Masanobu) and Nishimura (mainly Toyonobu). The schematization with weaker expression on those sheets was, of course, not caused by less talent on the part of the artists, as Rumpf asserted. It is rather more indicative of the fact that the monumental style, created in the first quarter of the eighteenth century, was a dead end with no possibility of development. Torii II could not intensify the bombastic grandeur of the figures created by his predecessors, without reaching absurdity. He tried, on the contrary, to give the style more reasonable proportions. In doing so, however, he suppressed its basic character and what remained was but a mere scheme, as we can see on some of the sheets from the thirties.

It seems that some artists noticed this dead end of the monumental woodcuts. For that reason perhaps Nishimura Shigenaga used woodcuts for experiments on other subjects: flowers, birds, landscapes. For that reason perhaps Nishikawa Sukenobu sought a different way in his pictures of geishas. I dare express the opinion that this difference was not caused by his living in a different environment, i. e., in Kyoto and Osaka. In his early works from around the year 1720 one can see that he, too, tried in composition and line to apply the 'monumental' style, like his Edo colleagues (see the women in the book *Sanjuni-so Sugata Kurabe* from the year 1717).

The changes in orientation should rather be ascribed to his artistic instinct, which led him to adopt a line of creation that was called conservative but which opened the way for the entire further development of his art.

V SUKENOBU AND KIYOMITSU

Transition to a New Scheme

To understand the woodcut of the forties and fifties of the eighteenth century we must return to Sukenobu, to his books from the twenties and later. They contained chiefly pictures of women, a subject that always was in the van of the development of Japanese woodcuts. In the epilogue to the book *Ehon Tokiwagusa* (Osaka 1720), Sukenobu laid down instructions how to paint pictures of women, and these instructions are at the same time his personal credo. For pictures of ladies at court he suggested a realistic conception, i. e., a study of the fashion and the structure of the human body before the figure is robed in garments. For pictures of courtesans he recommended an expression of the natural beauties of the body without formal hindrances. In the book *Ehon Yamato Hiji* (Kyoto, 1742) he once more proclaimed his principles of painting, mainly his faith in the greatness of the Japanese national culture and the national tradition of painting.

His work is truly marked by certain trends which might be called classicism. This can be seen in the composition, which by again using architectural elements in the background returned consistently to the yamato-e principles. The same is true of the drawing which in each stroke shows honest brushwork technique. For these qualities Sukenobu was highly esteemed by contemporary critics and Kenji Toda quotes this statement by scholar and painter Yanagisawa Rikyo (1706–1758): 'Hanabusa Itcho is good at painting ukiyo-e. There are also painters like Okumura Masanobu, Torii Kiyonobu, Hagawa Chincho and Kaigetsudo, but the master is Nishikawa Sukenobu. Sukenobu is the saint of ukiyo-e.'

At the same time certain elements on his pictures belong to the sphere of

64

realism; such as his endeavours to express forms and relations as precisely as possible and avoiding any exaggeration in drawing or proportions. (Such efforts cannot be seen in the work of, e. g., Torii Kiyonobu.) The realistic attitude can be found also in his selection of themes from all spheres of human activities. Of course there are certain elements, too, that stand in contrast to the demands of realism, such as his creation of types and idealized figures which should be ascribed mainly to the other extreme of his endeavour to give the pictures poetic, romantic content.

In view of his further development this matter of content is an important part of Sukenobu's woodcuts. Kiyonobu glorified the life in the town, Sukenobu made it a topic for poetry. I do not believe that this was caused simply by his working in the most highly cultured environment of Kamigata. The cause lay presumably in his anticipation of the most progressive features of the subsequent development. Kiyonobu depicted the town at a time when the new-rich bourgeoisie was trying with primitive bombast to imitate the debauchery and conceit of the lazy and degenerate samurai. The new leading class first adopted the bad manners of the defeated élite. Sukenobu, on the contrary, spoke for the bourgeoisie that intended to test its victory by taking over the national culture and acquiring the good manners of the defeated élite.

In the woodcuts of the Edo school romantic content appeared for the first time about 1740, thanks mainly to the workshop of Okumura Masanobu. In his illustrations and hand-painted sheets after 1745 and in his two-coloured prints the previously arrogant gestures are replaced by a warmth of feeling, relaxed, natural behaviour and a mood of melancholic nostalgia. In style he followed the Okumuro tradition from the beginning of the century, but the rhythm of the lines is far more subdued and softer, the design of the draperies strikes the eye less blatantly, and the background is filled up with increasing numbers of small details. The woodcut returned consistently to the perspective seen obliquely from above and to smaller figures. Our illustrations from the erotic album *Neya-no Hinagata* from the year 1739 (see plate 30) shows Masanobu's success in transition to the new attunement. But the change in style is not yet so clearly visible as, e. g., on the magnificent triptych of 'Lovers under an Umbrella' in the Stocklet Col-

lection (compare B. Moddeman, *Oude Japansche Prentkunst*, Catalogue of the Gemente Museum, The Hague, 1938, p. 14, pl. 4), or in the picture by Kikugoro, in the Kanda Collection (Noguchi, op. cit., pl. 79). It seems that Masanobu's success even stimulated Ishikawa Toyonobu to work in a similar manner; his 'Girl Reading a Book of Love Poems' (ibid., pl. 76), some excellent prints in the Ledoux Collection, or the painting in our collection (plate 37), reach the level of the above-mentioned works by Masanobu.

In the Torii school the change in style took place in close connection with changes in technique, or, correctly speaking, as a consequence of these changes.

On the two-coloured prints, which Torii II began to publish some time after 1743, this change is not yet consistent. Only the bombast of forms and movements gradually faded away, and the necessity of composing with only two colours and black gave these sheets a more restrained appearance in comparison with the polychromy of the hand-coloured sheets (see plate 27). A visible change in content and form can be seen only with the appearance of sheets signed Torii III – Kiyomitsu. The latter took over the position as leading master in the workshop after 1752.

Other sheets that show these changes have the following signatures: Kiyohiro, Kiyotsune, Kiyotada. I am thinking of prints with two to five colours on which the figures became longer and thinner and where the yamato-e scheme influenced the increased use of architectural forms in the background and the more elaborate setting, and where the expression and motion of the figure became increasingly elegant (compare plates 27 and 28). On comparing these sheets by Kiyomitsu with the grandiose impression made by the woodcuts of his predecessors in the period 1710 to 1740, a decline is visible. But if we consider them one stage on the road leading ahead to Harunobu, they are an advance. And it could not be otherwise, for the town and the people for whom the woodcuts were intended had not yet retreated from the position they had won during the first half of the century. So far they were marching ahead, even if not with such pioneering spirit as their ancestors of 1710.

70

In summing up the development of the Japanese woodcut in its earliest phase my first task is to explain why I avoided the term 'Primitives', which used to be applied to the masters of Japanese engraving in the period under consideration. The first reason is that the Japanese themselves criticize this term, for it must seem to refer to primitive creations of Japanese society before it became civilized. In fact, at this period the civilization and culture of Japan had reached a very high level of development. At the time when Moronobu, Kiyonobu and Masanobu were at work, the painters Korin, Sumiyoshi Kukei, and Kano Tsunenobu were famous.

At that time ceramic production was of a high standard in Japan, lacquer work at its most exquisite and architecture most perfect. Chikamatsu was writing dramas and Basho composing poems. Nor was the technique of engraving at a primitive stage of development; on the contrary, it could already look back on centuries of experience. Perhaps only the *élan* and the instinctive energy in which the rising power of the bourgeois society found its artistic expression, might be called 'primitive'. Such is the *élan* of every rising young nation, young ethnical group, young class in society. But the development through which this young society and its art passed is too complex a form of phenomenon to be encompassed in one term.

I have tried on the basis of technique, theme, style and content to divide the woodcuts into continuous and, wherever possible, self-contained periods. I have reached the conclusion that such periods *can* be distinguished.

In the initial period (up to 1600) the conditions were being created in technique and style for the subsequent development of the woodcut. The first outstanding woodcuts made their appearance in the period 1600–1660. They had secular themes and helped to popularize the classical heritage of the national culture. In the third period (1660–1710) the woodcuts reflected the interests of the city population as expressed in the so-called genre themes. The style of the woodcut was radically changing. In the fourth period (1710–1740) this society expressed its victory and self-awareness in bombastic creations, a grandiose, monumental style

stressed further by new technical requisites. (Tan-e, Beni-e, Urushi-e). The fifth period (1740–1765) is a transitional stage. The society in the cities was preparing to take over the leading positions of responsibility and to develop the national culture. The woodcut returned to the classical canons of style, to the traditional poetical contents of a picture. The technique was transferred to multi-coloured prints as a transitional stage towards full polychromy.

CATALOGUE

BUDDHIST PRINTS AND YAMATO-E

(For data regarding the development of these prints and pictures see Chapters I and II.)

Page 18. A Votive Picture with 33 Buddhist Gods.
Inscription: The Nachi Monastery in Kumano, Kii Province. Black-and-white print. Kakemono-e size: 58×21 cm. (Mounted on paper with mica ornaments). 16th–17th century (?). J. Hloucha Collection in Prague.

Page 22. Genre Scene.
Hand-coloured printed fan, used as background for a Hoke-kyo Sutra text. Width: 10.7×25.3 cm. Second half of 12th century. Reproduced from the catalogue, *National Treasures of Japan*, series I, 1951.

Page 31. Prince and his Suite.
Illustration to the *Ise Monogatari* edition published 1608. 27×19 cm. Reproduced from J. Kurth: *Masterpieces of Japanese Woodcuts*.

Page 35. A Legendary Scene.
From a religious biography. In style close to the illustrations of Nichiren Shonin Chu-ga-san from 1632 and to the early illustrations by the Kyoto designer, Hinaya Ryuho. Black-and-white print. Book illustration, size of page approx. 19×14 cm. 1630–1650. Collection of the National Gallery in Prague.

Plate 1. Picture of a Dragon.
Inscription: Shuin Monastery, Shinano Province. Hand-coloured in vermilion red. Aiban size: 33 × 21 cm. (Mounted on paper with mica ornaments). Beginning of 17th century (?). J. Hloucha Collection.

Plates 2 and 3. Two details from a Buddhist woodcut print.
From the Tenno-ji temple in Osaka. Stencilled print kappa-zuri-e. Kakemono-e size: 71 × 24 cm. 18th cent. print copied from an earlier picture. J. Hloucha Collection in Prague.

Plates 4 and 5. Picnic.
Details of outdoor genre scenes on a folding screen. The main picture shows a picnic in the open air and servants preparing the food. On the lower section the guests are arriving on horseback and by boat. The upper section shows a landscape. The upper and lower edges are covered with a horizontal strip of clouds, which is also found between the upper and central sections. No signature. Painted and gilded on paper. Byobu-e, 144 × 153 cm. Second half of 17th century. Collection of the National Gallery in Prague.

Plate 6. Nara-bon: *Ehon Waka-shu*.
32 sheets, without numbers. Each page was separately attached to folded paper which was then sewn into book form. The linen cover has the inscription *Ehon Waka-shu*. Each page contains three illustrations painted in the shape of a fan and the text of poems. 39 × 27 cm. End of 16th century. Collection of the National Gallery in Prague.

Plates 7–11. Screen with Genre Pictures.
Scenes of the four noble forms of entertainment (music, chess, painting and calligraphy). Woodcut reproduction from the 19th century based on the 17th century *Hikone-byobu* of the Ii collection. Byobu-e, 65 × 190 cm. J. Hloucha Collection in Prague.

THE SCHOOL OF MORONOBU

Hishikawa Kichibei Fujiwara Moronobu was born in the village of Hota, Awa province, about two hours' journey from Tokyo. The year of his birth is given in different sources as 1618, 1625 or 1638. His grandfather Shichiemon and his father Kichiemon Michishige worked in Hota as dyers and embroiderers of textiles. Moronobu also learnt this trade and worked as a pattern designer even when he later moved to Edo. There he became a student of painting in the schools of Tosa and Kano and possibly also in Iwasa Matabei school. At a later date he established his own workshop. He must have been an untiring worker if one is to judge by the illustrations in the 150 books ascribed to him. Noguchi is of the opinion that Moronobu's first work are the illustrations in the book *Buncho-zoshi*, published in 1650, and that his style of painting reached maturity towards the end of the sixties. In 1694 Moronobu abandoned work and became a monk. This is confirmed by an inscription on a bell which Moronobu had cast on that occasion for the Rinkaizan Hetsugan monastery in his native village of Hota. The inscription reads: 'Presented by Hishikawa Kichibei no jo Fujiwara Moronobu, Nyudo Yuchiku on this happy day of the fifth month of the seventh year in the Genroku era, the Year of the Dog.' It appears that he died very soon afterwards, for the epilogue to the book *Furyu Sugatae Hyakunin Isshu* ('Fashionable Portraits for the Collection of One Hundred Poets', published in May 1695) states that these pictures by Moronobu found in the house of his son Morofusa were published posthumously in honour of the artist (see *Ryerson Collection*, p. 110). The question as to who exactly should be included in Moronobu's school has never been entirely clarified. His son Hishikawa Morofusa left a number of woodcuts from around 1790, none of which are on a high artistic level. One of his outstanding disciples was probably Tarobei Furuyama Moroshige, who worked chiefly in the nineties of the 17th century. Sugimura Jihei may also have worked in Moronobu's studio. He was a gifted painter who sank more or less into complete oblivion. In the seventies of the 17th century he is said to have been as famous as Moronobu and to have produced a great deal of work during the following decades which is wrongly ascribed to Moronobu. His re-discovery some time ago is due to the Japanese scholar K. Shibui.

Tradition labelled Torii Kiyonobu I as one of Moronobu's disciples, but Rumpf has expressed doubts on this point. But it seems likely that for some time Okumura Masonobu worked in Moronobu's studio. The relation of painters Kaigetsudo Ando, Kondo Kiyoharu and Hanegawa Chincho to Moronobu's school remains enigmatic.

Page 41. Two Knights.
No signature. Print coloured red by hand (now yellow-brown). Book illustration, size 18.2 × 16.5 cm. The hair-style indicates the period between 1670 and 1680. Collection of the National Gallery in Prague.

Page 42. Love Scene.
Signature Jihei (Sugimura) on the man's belt. One of the series of erotic sheets by Sugimura Jihei (see Shibui: Catalogue No. 94, pl. XIII). Sumi-e print. Oban yoke-e size: 28.5 × 38.5 cm. 1690–1700. J. Hloucha Collection in Prague.

Page 46. Knight in the Company of Three Courtesans.
Signed Kiri (Sugimura Jihei) on the knight's drapery. Sumi-e print. Oban yoko-e size: 27 × 39 cm. 1690–1700. J. Hloucha Collection in Prague.

Plates 12–14. The Girls' Quarter.
Signed Nihon Eshi-sen Hishikawa Hitsu. Moronobu's stamp. Sign of Choji-ya house on the curtain. Painted on paper in Indian ink and colours. Size 35 × 43 cm. mounted as kakemono-e. Judging by hair-style and dress a late work from the period around 1690. J. Hloucha Collection in Prague.

Plate 15. Shamisen Player and Listener.
No signature, in style close to the work of Furuyama Moroshige. Painted on paper in ink and colours. Size 21 × 40 cm. mounted as kakemono-e. 1690–1700. J. Hloucha Collection in Prague.

Plate 16. Festive Races.
Inscribed Fukaki Matsuri. Text describing the Mongol invasion of Japan in 1279, no signature. Hand-coloured print (red, yellow). Two pages in one, size of picture 22×33 cm. 1670–1680. Collection of the National Gallery in Prague.

TORII I AND II

In the history of Japanese woodcuts the Torii family represents a Great Power, for they have been designing woodcuts ever since the 17th century and still do so today. Japanese and European scholars are on the whole agreed on the early stages of this family. The first known member was Torii Shoshichi who as an actor assumed the name Nakamura Jugoro, and as a painter of theatre posters called himself Torii Kiyotaka or Kiyomoto. From 1645 on he lived first in Osaka, where he played female roles on the stage, and in spring 1687 he moved to Edo, where he settled near the theatre street in Naniwacho and began to act in heroic parts. From 1690 on he painted posters for the Ichimura-za Theatre and died in 1702. Reports say that he studied painting in Kyoto under the painter Kiyochika, a pupil of Miyasaki Yuzen. None of his work is known now; he probably did not take up woodcuts, and it would seem that the founders of the woodcut tradition in his family came after him.

But there is great confusion in regard to these descendants whom we have called Torii I and II for the purposes of this book – according to signatures most frequently found: Torii Kiyonobu and Torii Kiyomasu. Kiyonobu was first marked as Torii I, Kiyomasu as Torii II (e.g., in J. Kurth's work). Kiyomasu was considered Kiyonobu's son (in Kurth's work, his brother). A more recent Japanese genealogy worked out by Inoue Kazuo and used by Yone Noguchi distinguishes four Toriis in the first half of the 18th century, Kiyonobu I and II and Kiyomasu I and II. The German scholar F. Rumpf reached different conclusions on the basis of studying the family chronicle, the tombstones of the Torii family and by dating several sheets with actors according to actors' almanacs and chronicles (see OAZ 1930, p. 16–31). I follow his information on the first two masters of the Torii school, bearing in mind, however, that the facts and conclusions reached by him have not yet been completely confirmed.

The Torii style in woodcuts was founded by a certain Shobei who was born in 1664 and married in 1693 into the Torii family. He began to use the signature Torii Shobei, after 1700 Torii Kiyonobu, and from 1704 on also Torii Kiyomasu. (Rumpf's dates must be wrong, as in the Chicago Collection there is a collection of short stories with the signature Torii Kiyomasu from the year 1696). He is said to have been a disciple of Moronobu's, and we can really trace some similarity of style in his early works. Rumpf is of the opinion that he was taught by his father-in-law Shoshichi, especially in regard to his works with topics from the theatrical world. The stamp 'Iwasa', discovered on some of his pictures, shows his connection with the Matabei school. Torii's I work was centred around theatrical themes; he also painted women, erotic sheets and historical as well as legendary subjects and pictures of animals. In 1727 he relinquished the management of his studio and died in 1729.

The management of his studio was taken over by his disciple Shojiro, born in 1706. He, too, married in 1724 into the Torii family, took over from his master and father-in-law the name of Kiyonobu. From 1727 on he was the head of the studio (after that year the signature Nidaime Torii, i. e., Torii II, appeared on some sheets), and after the death of his father-in-law he began to use also the name of Kiyomasu. Most of his subjects are taken from the theatrical world. In the forties he began to issue two-coloured woodcuts; in 1752 he retired from the management of the studio, where he was followed by his son (Torii Kiyomitsu), and died in 1763.

According to Rumpf, Torii I (Shobei) and Torii II (Shojiro) used the name of Kiyonobu as well as Kiyomasu. While both were working at the same time, i. e., in the twenties, Shobei signed himself Kiyomasu, and

Shojiro, Kiyonobu. He claims to distinguish differences in style, which, however, in my opinion, do not seem at all apparent during this critical period.

In this period of the twenties the signatures Torii Kiyotomo, Torii Kiyotada and Torii Kiyoshige can be found. We do not know whether these were members of the family or pupils. Comparisons of style and manners of signing might even lead to the conclusion that these are yet further names of the two Torii: one of our sheets (see pl. 17) has only the word Torii as signature. It is possible that only two Torii painters existed in the first half of the 18th century. A second possibility is that there may have been seven or even more. So far no definite proof has been given. Nor has the dividing line between the work of the two painters, Torii I and Torii II, been definitely established, though one might safely ascribe the work before 1720 to the first master and that after 1730 to the second. That is the reason why in this volume all the sheets of the Torii school from the middle of the 18th century have been given under one heading, Torii I and II.

Plate 17. Actor Tsugawa Kamon in a Female Part.
This sheet was published in honour of the actor's arrival in Edo. Signed: Torii Hitsu. Publisher: Komatsu-ya. Urushi-e print with gold dust. Hoso-e size: 27.5 × 15 cm.
The precise date of this event is not known to me. The style places the sheet in the 1720–1725 period. There is an actor with the same mark on his sleeve on Kiyonobu's sheet in the Arts and Crafts Museum in Berlin (Kurth, *Die Primitiven des Japanholzschnitts*, pl. 18). No name is given. F. Rumpf, *Meister*, p. 22, calls this actor Mizuki Takejuro and dates the sheet in the period around 1710. Rumpf's identification is probably incorrect as the actor is almost certainly Kamon, who probably appeared as a guest artist on the Edo stage not only about 1710 but also later. Collection of the National Gallery in Prague. (Our sheet was described by Kurth, *Geschichte*, vol. I, page 203. The outline of the head is given there as illustr. No. 25).

Plate 18. Actor Sodezaki Iseno in the Role of a Geisha.
Signed: Eshi Torii Kiyomasu Hitsu. Publisher: Urokagata-ya, Edo.

Urushi-e print with gold dust. Hoso-e size: 32.3 × 15.2 cm. 1730 to 1740. National Gallery in Prague. (This sheet, which was formerly in the Jaekel Collection, is described by Kurth, *Geschichte*, vol. I, page 220).

Plate 19. Actor Sanogawa Mangiku (1690–1747) in a Female Role and Actor Fujimura Hanjuro (male parts since 1729) in a Male Role. Signed: Torii Kiyomasu Hitsu. Publisher: Mato-Hama-cho Nakajima-ya. Urushi-e print with gold dust. Hoso-e size: 33.3 × 15.5 cm. 1730–1740. Collection of the National Gallery in Prague.

Plate 20. Travelling Sheet Miyage-e. Title: Autumn Moon on Mount Ishiyama, sixth sheet from the serial 'Eight Views of Omi' *(Omi Hakkei)*. Signed: Eshi Torii Kiyonobu Hitsu. Publisher: Iga-ya, Edo. Urushi-e print. Hoso-e size: 33.5 × 15.8 cm. About 1730. Collection of the National Gallery, Prague.

Plate 21. Knight on Horseback. Signed: Torii Kiyoshige. Publisher: Nakajima-ya. Coloured urushi-e print with gold dust. Hoso-e size: 32.3 × 15.2 cm. 1730–1740. Collection of the National Gallery in Prague. (Compare this sheet with the one signed Kiyonobu in the Rex Collection, Kurth, *Der Japanische Holzschnitt*, Berlin 1922, illustr. 15).

Plates 22 and 23. Actor Sawamura Sojuro (1689–1756) in a Heroic Part. Signed: Torii Kiyomasu Hitsu. Publisher: Okamura-ya. Stamp of Collector Hayashi Tadamasa. Coloured beni-e print. Hoso-e size: 31.4 × 15 cm. About 1730. Collection of the National Gallery in Prague.

Plate 24. Actor Yamashita Kinsaku (active from 1739–1750) in a Female Role in the Play *Yukihiro and the Fishing Women Matsukaze and Murasame*. Signed: Torii Kiyomasu Hitsu. Publisher: Iga-ya, Edo. Urushi-e print with gold dust. Hoso-e size: 30 × 16.2 cm. 1730–1740. Collection of the National Gallery in Prague.

Plate 25. Actors Sawamura Sojuro (1689–1756) and Sakata Hangoro II (1734–1782) in Heroic Parts.
Signed: Torii Kiyonobu Hitsu. Publisher: Enami-ya. Two-coloured beni-e print. Hoso-e size: 30.3 × 14.6 cm. About 1750. Collection of the National Gallery in Prague.

Plate 26. Actors Ichikawa Ebizo (Danjuro II, 1688–1758) and Nakamura Sukegoro (1739–1763) in Heroic Parts.
Signed: Torii Kiyomasu Hitsu. Publisher: Uemura (?). Two-coloured beni-e print. Hoso-e size: 27.8 × 13.6 cm. About 1750. Collection of the National Gallery in Prague.

Plate 27. Actors Sawamura Sojuro II (1750–1770) and Matsumoto Koshiro (1735–1754) in the roles of Otokodate Knights.
Signed: Torii Kiyomasu Hitsu. Publisher: Yamato Maru-ya. Two-coloured beni-e print. Hoso-e size: 28 × 13.3 cm. About 1750. National Gallery in Prague.

THE SCHOOL OF OKUMURA MASANOBU

Some books give 1690 as Okumura Masanobu's year of birth and 1768 as the year in which he died. Since his first illustrated books originated in the years 1701–1704 he was considered an infant prodigy who already at the age of eleven masterfully painted pictures of courtesans. Rumpf's thorough investigation into all these facts showed that Masanobu must have been at least 60 years old in 1708, and thus he reached more plausible dates about the Okumura school, which in the absence of other proofs should be accepted. (See OAZ, 1930, pp. 87–99).
The founder of the school was Okumura Gempachi Shimmyo Masa-

nobu, who lived from about 1649 to 1711, using at times the poetical names of Baio and Baigin. He probably was a disciple of Moronobu, and after the latter's death he probably worked in Torii Kiyonobu's workshop. (But certainly not as a student since he was fifteen years older). In the period from 1701 to 1711 he published over 30 albums and illustrated books, which in the initial period he signed with the name of Okumura Gempachi Masanobu, after 1703 only Okumura Masanobu, and from 1707 on Okumura Shimmyo Masanobu.

The dates 1690–1768 concern his son, who in 1715–1718 signed his woodcuts Okumura Genroku, and later Okumura Masanobu. He also used the poetical names of Shimmyo, later Tanchosai, Kukujudo and Hogetsudo. About the year 1725 he founded his own publishing house in Edo under the name of Okumura-ya.

Okumura Toshinobu was the son, perhaps, of Okumura Gempachi Masanobu, as is stated in some sources, and the brother of Okumura Genroku. But these names may have been used by one and the same person. The name Toshinobu can be found from 1718 to 1736. Okumura Bunshi Masafusa was also a pupil and perhaps even the son of Okumura Gempachi. His data are unknown.

Page 51. Girl Entertaining Three Men by Playing the Shamisen (detail). No signature. Sumi-e print. Oban yoko-e size: 29.3 × 40.5 cm. About 1710. Collection of the National Gallery in Prague.

Page 54. Self-portrait of Okumura Masanobu.
Signed Okumura Masanobu Hitsu. One version of this sheet (containing text instead of landscape and signature on the screen) was printed in 1707 in the series *Ukiyo Fuzoku Okashii Koto-Fukuro*. Our version appeared later. The coat has the sign Ju. Sumi-e print. Oban yoko-e size: 29.4 × 40.3 cm. About 1710. Collection of the National Gallery in Prague.

Page 57. Legendary Scene (detail).
No signature. Sumi-e print. Oban yoko-e size: 29.4 × 40.5 cm. About 1710. Collection of the National Gallery in Prague.

Page 59. Walk in the Snow.
Title: Ironi Tsumoru Hagi-no Shirotae. No signature. Sumi-e print.
Page from a book, 22.5×14 cm. 1740–1750. J. Hloucha Collection in
Prague.

Plate 28. Actor Arashi Wakano (1727) in the Role of a Flower Girl.
Signed: Gako Okumura Toshinobu Hitsu. Publisher: Izutsu-ya. Urushi-e
print with gold dust. Hoso-e size: 29.8×15.3 cm. About 1725. Collection
of the National Gallery in Prague.

Plate 29. Tatsuoka Hisagiku in the Role of Matsukaze in the Play about
Yukihiro.
No signature and no indication of publisher. The mark Masa in the rhom-
bus probably indicates the authorship of Masanobu and his publishing
house, Okumura-ya, as publisher. Coloured print. Hoso-e size: 32×14.8 cm.
About 1738. Collection of the National Gallery in Prague.
(A sheet by Kiyonobu with the same actor in the same role was published
on the occasion of Hisagiku's moving to Edo). Noguchi places him in
the period around 1734. (See *Ukiyo-e Primitives*, Plate 33). But it is known
that Tatsuoka acted in Edo from 1738–1742.

Plate 30. Love Letter.
Sheet from Masanobu's album *Some Iro no Yama*, *Neya-no Hinagata*,
with the poem: Scent of the Plum Blossom,
Oh, the scent of your lips,
The scent of the breath,
The scent of the first smile of the year.
Coloured print. (In the Shibui collection the same sheet exists as urushi-e.
See Noguchi, *Ukiyo-e Primitives*, plate 58, and Ledoux Collection, *The Pri-
mitives*, pl. 23). Oban yoko-e size: 24.5×36.5 cm. 1739. J. Hloucha
Collection in Prague.

Plate 31. Entertainment by Girls.
Sheet No. 10 from *Hokuri Yugijo* ('Entertainments in the Northern

Quarter'). Three-coloured beni-e print (the same album was published earlier in black-and-white; this edition appeared about 1755). Oban yoko-e size: 25.5×37 cm. Private collection in Prague.

Plate 32 and page 52. Geisha from Edo.
Inscription: Centre of Triptych, Yoshiwara, Snow. Signed: Yamato Gako Okumura Toshinobu Hitsu. Publisher: Izutsu-ya. Urushi-e print. Hoso-e size: 32×15.5 cm. 1720–1730. Collection of the National Gallery in Prague. (The same sheet in different colouring can be found in the Succo Collection. See Kurth: *Masterpieces of Japanese Woodcuts*, plate 6.)

THE NISHIMURA SCHOOL

In the first half of the 18th century two painters of the Nishimura school worked as designers for woodcuts. Though in older books various identifications are given for them, more recent opinion among Japanese and European scholars has come to the same conclusions about the personalities of the two painters. Nishimura Shigenaga was born in 1697 in Edo. His teacher is unknown, but judging by his early style it was probably Okumura Gempachi Masanobu. The oldest works known to have come from his hand are illustrations to stories about dead souls *(Shiryo Gedatsu Monogatari)*, published in 1712 *(Ryerson Collection*, p. 164.)

In contrast to other designers his themes ranged over a very broad field. Sheets are known with pictures of birds, landscapes and Buddhist subjects. About 1740 he followed Masanobu in painting sheets with European perspective (uki-e). There are no colour prints of his from the forties and later; he died in 1756. Side by side with the name of Nishimura Shigenaga he also used the names of Sentado and Eigado.

Ishikawa Toyonobu, his disciple, was born in Edo in the year 1711.

In 1730 he began to publish woodcuts signed Nishimura Magasaburo, and from 1737–38 until 1744 his sheets bear the signature Nishimura Shige-nobu. Then he began to publish two-coloured woodcuts and changed his name to Ishikawa Toyonobu. In civil life he used the name Ishikawa Shichibei, and the poetical pseudonyms Tanjodo and Shuha. He was still active at work in the sixties of the seventieth century when he, like other artists, succumbed to the Harunobu influence. He died in 1785, or, according to different sources, in 1768. The school of Nishimura Shigenaga includes also other masters of the woodcut, such as, for instance, Harunobu, Eishosai, Nagayoshi, and Nagahide in Osaka, and others. Most of them, however, worked at a later period.

Frontispiece: Actor of the Arashi Family in Various Roles.
Anonymous sheet in memoriam by an artist of the Nishimura or Okumura school. (The *mon* of Kiri was used by the family Nakayama in the second half of the 18th century. Earlier it was used perhaps by some actors of the Nakamura and Arashi families. Our picture probably shows Monjuro.) Sumi-e print. Hoso-e size: 33 × 14.5 cm. 1730–1740. J. Hloucha Collection in Prague.

Plate 33. Gigwa – Humorous Picture with the God of Happiness, Hotei. Signed: Nishimura Shigenaga. Publisher: Iga-ya. Urushi-e print with gold dust. Hoso-e size: 30.7 × 15.7 cm. 1720–1730. Collection of the National Gallery in Prague.

Plate 34. Byobu-e – Picture with motif of birds to be pasted on a screen. Signed: Yamato-e Nishimura Shigenaga Hitsu. Publisher: Urokogata-ya. Hand-coloured beni-e print. Hoso-e size: 24.8 × 14 cm. About 1725. Collection of the National Gallery in Prague.

Plate 35. Byobu-e – Sheet with motif of cobwebs to be pasted on a screen. Signed: Eshi Nishimura Shigenaga Hitsu with Shigenaga's stamp. Publisher: Izumi-ya Gonshiro. Hand-coloured beni-e print. Hoso-e size: 31.5 × 15 cm. About 1725. Collection of the National Gallery in Prague.

Plate 36. Actor Ishikawa Danjuro II (d. 1758) in the Role of Soga no Goro and Actor Segawa Kikunojo (1691–1749) in the Role of the Girl Shosho.
Signed: Nishimura Magasaburo. Publisher: Urokogata-ya. Stamps of collectors Hayashi and Wakai Oyaji. Urushi-e print with gold dust. Hoso-e size: 33×15.5 cm. 1730–1735. (Danjuro II adopted the name of Ebizo I in 1735.) Collection of the National Gallery in Prague. (This sheet was mentioned by the Sotheby Catalogue, June 1911, No. 13, and by Kurth, *Geschichte*, vol. I, page 319).

Plate 37; pages 70 and 71. Serenade.
Signed: Ishikawa Toyonobu. Stamp not readable. Ink and colour painting on paper. Naga-e size: 99×11.5 cm. About 1760. J. Hloucha Collection, Prague.

NISHIKAWA SUKENOBU

The schools of Torii, Okumura and Nishimura developed the tradition of woodcuts in Edo. In the Kamigata district (the area around Kyoto and Osaka) the outstanding master in woodcuts in the first half of the eighteenth century was Nishikawa Sukenobu. This painter was born in 1671 (or 1678) in Kyoto, studied figure painting under Kano Eino and Tosa Mitsusuke. In 1710 he set up his own studio and school in Kyoto, and later in Osaka. Since the Kyoto public preferred woodcuts in books to loose sheets he did not design such sheets. The first books with his illustrations appeared in 1710. (Shibui, *Estampes Érotiques*, cites on pp. 13–17 four titles from the years 1710–1711 and six more before 1715). His entire work consists of over one hundred titles (sometimes as many as 300 are cited). His greatest contribution were pictures of women and he frequently drew illustrations to classical works. The book 'One Hundred Different Types of Women' *(Hyakunin Joro Shina Sadame)*, (Kyoto, 1723) is considered his best work, but other books rival this fame, such as his *Ehon Tokiwagusa*, (Osaka 1720), *Ehon Chiomigusa*, (Osaka, 1740) and *Ehon Yamato Hiji*, (Kyoto, 1742). He died in 1751, leaving behind a large number of disciples and imitators. Rumpf (*Meister*, p. 106) names 12 of his pupils in Kyoto, three in Osaka and three in Edo.

His most outstanding disciples are perhaps Takagi Sadatake, Hasegawe Mitsunobu and Shimokoba Shusui.

Page 60. The Hero Asahino.
Sheet from an album or book. (A sheet from the same collection is cited by Rumpf in *Sammlung Tony Straus–Negbaur*, Berlin, 1928, No. 121). Signed: Yamato Eshi Nishikawa Sukenobu Hitsu. Sumi-e print. Sheet cut down to size: 26.3 × 17.9 cm. 1710–1720. Collection of the National Gallery, Prague.

Page 61. The Hero Asahino Fighting.
Sheet from the same album as the preceding. Signed: Yamato Eshi Nishikawa Sukenobu Hitsu. Sumi-e print. Sheet cut down to size: 26.6 × 18 cm. 1710–1720. Collection of the National Gallery in Prague.

Plates 38 and 39. Court Lady Raising a Curtain and Geisha with Servant Girl. Published as frontispieces to the first and second volume of the book *Hyakunin Joro Shina Sadame* ('One Hundred Types of Women'), published in Kyoto by Hachimonjiya Hachisaemon in the year 1723 with an introduction by Hachimonjiya Jisho. Hand-coloured print. Book page: 23.8 × 17.8 cm. 1723. Collection of the National Gallery in Prague.

Page 64. Daimo's Concubine and her Companion at a Country House (detail). Sheets 10–11 of the first volume of the same book. Collection of the National Gallery in Prague.

Page 65. The Courtesan Tsubone-Joro.
Sheets 7–8 of the second volume of the same book. Collection of the National Gallery in Prague.

Page 67. Courtesan with Governess at her Toilet (detail).
Sheets 3–4 of the second volume of the same book. Collection of the National Gallery in Prague.

Page 68. Apprentices and Servants (detail).
Sheets 12–13 of the first volume of the same book. Collection of the National Gallery in Prague.

Page 73. Kumi-ya – Rope-makers (detail).
Sheets 18–19 of the first volume of the same book. Collection of the National Gallery in Prague.

Plate 40. Page from an erotic book (shunga).
Signed: Takewara ga. Perhaps by Takehara Shunchosai. J. Kurth (*Geschichte*, vol. I, p. 422 ff.) cites another shunga with the same signature on the first page and with an introduction by Sukenobu. According to its style, this print belongs definitely to the Sukenobu school. Three-coloured beni-e print. Size: 26×17 cm. 1750–1760. Collection of the National Gallery in Prague.

TORII III

Torii II Shojiro had several disciples whose names can be found in sheets from the fifties and sixties of the 17th century. They include Kiyo-shiro Kiyotada II and Kiyomitsu. Kiyomitsu was his second son, born in the year 1735, who took over the management of the studio in 1752 and himself retired in 1785. The work of this Torii III and his co-students falls into the time when the printed woodcuts developed from two-coloured prints into polychrome brocade prints (nishiki-e). Kiyomitsu used four colours in about 1762 and went over to polychrome prints at the same time as Harunobu in about 1765. The themes of the Torii workshop were selected chiefly from the world of the theatre. Kiyomitsu had several pupils, among them Kiyotsune and Kiyonaga.

Plate 41. Lady with Servants on a Walk.
Signed: Torii Kiyomitsu Hitsu and Kiyomitsu's stamp. Publisher (?) known only by his address: Moto-ishi-cho. Two-coloured beni-e print. Chuban size: 28×20 cm. 1750–1755. J. Hloucha Collection in Prague.

Plate 42. Actor Otani Hiroji (1747–1757) in the Heroic Part of Sokada no Kanetoki.
Signed: Torii Kiyomitsu Ga. Publisher: Matsumura-ya. Three-coloured print. Hoso-e size: 11.1×13.7 cm. About 1760. Collection of the National Gallery in Prague.

Plate 43. The actor Otani Hiroji (1747–1757) in a Heroic Part.
Signed: Torii Kiyomitsu Ga. Publisher: Mori-ya Jihei. Three-coloured print. Hoso-e size: 30.8×14.1 cm. About 1760. Collection of the National Gallery in Prague.

Plate 44. The actor Segawa Kikunojo II (1756–1773) in the role of a mountain woman from the Agara Hills.
Signed: Torii Kiyomitsu Ga. Publisher: Iwato-ya. Three-coloured print. Hoso-e size: 29.6×13.5 cm. About 1765. Collection of the National Gallery in Prague.

Plate 45. The actor Onoue Kikugoro (1717–1782) in a Female Role. Without signature and without publisher's stamp. Probably by Torii Kiyomitsu. Three-coloured print. Hoso-e size: 30.7×14.1 cm. About 1760. Collection of the National Gallery in Prague.

Plate 46. The actor Bando Mitsugoro (1703–1782) in the Male Role of
Soga no Goro.
Signed: Torii Kiyomitsu Ga. Publisher: Takemiya-chi. Three-coloured
print. Hoso-e size: 30.6×13.9 cm. About 1770. (Actor Takeda Mino-
suke was adopted into the Bando family and took the name of Mitsugoro
in 1769). Collection of the National Gallery in Prague.

Plate 47. The actor Azuma Tozo in a Female Role.
Signed: Torii Kiyomitsu Ga. Publisher: Iwato-ya. Three-coloured print.
Hoso-e size: 31.6×13.3 cm. 1760–1765. Collection of the National
Gallery in Prague.

Plate 48. The actor Nakamura Tomijuro (1719–1786) in the Role of
a Geisha.
Signed: Torii Kiyohiro Hitsu. Publisher: Urokogata-ya. Two-coloured
beni-e print. Hoso-e size: 31.2×14.8 cm. About 1750. Collection of the
National Gallery in Prague.

Plate 49. The actor Matsumoto Koshiro III (1754–1770) in a Male Role.
Signed: Torii Kiyotsune Ga. Publisher: Omi-ya. Three-coloured print.
Hoso-e size: 31×13.5 cm. About 1770. J. Stříž Collection in Prague.

Plate 50. Girl Playing the Shamisen.
Signed: Torii Kiyomitsu Ga; Torii Kiyomitsu's stamp. Publisher: Maru-ya.
Three-coloured print. Naga-e size: 69.2×9.5 cm. 1760–1765. Collection
of the National Gallery in Prague.

BIBLIOGRAPHY

Aubert: Les maîtres de l'estampe japonaise. Paris 1930

Ausstellung Altjapanischer Kunst. Berlin 1939

Bachhofer L.: Die Kunst der Japanischen Holzschnittmeister. Munich 1922

Bernouilli R.: Ausgewählte Meisterwerke ostasiatischer Graphik in der Bibliothek für Kunst und Kunstgewerbe in Berlin. Plauen 1923

Binyon L.–J. J. O'Brien-Sexton: Japanese Colour Prints. London 1923

Boller W.: Meister des Japanischen Farbholzschnittes. Bern 1947

Catalogue Barboutau (Biographies des artistes japonais dont les oeuvres figurent dans la collection Barboutau. Tome II. Estampes et objets d'art). Paris 1904

Catalogue Gillot (Collection Ch. Gillot. II. partie: Estampes japonaises et livres illustrés). Paris 1914

Einstein: Der frühe japanische Holzschnitt. Berlin n. d.

Fenollosa E. F.: An Outline of the History of Ukiyo-e. Tokyo 1900

Fujikake Shizuya: An Introduction to Japanese Art. Tokyo 1936

Hillier J.: Japanese Masters of the Colour Print; A Great Heritage of Oriental Art. London 1954

Hilská V.: Dějiny a kultura japonského lidu. Prague 1954

Kenji Toda: Descriptive Catalogue of Japanese and Chinese Illustrated Books in the Ryerson Library of the Art Institute of Chicago. Chicago 1931

Kurth J.: Der Japanische Holzschnitt; Ein Abriss seiner Geschichte. Munich 1911, 1921, 1922

Kurth J.: Masterpieces of Japanese Woodcuts. Berlin 1924

Ledoux Collection: Primitives (Japanese Prints of the Primitive Period in the Collection of Louis V. Ledoux). New York 1942

Lemoisne O. A.: L'estampe japonaise. Paris n. d.

Minamoto H.: An Illustrated History of Japanese Art. Kyoto 1933

National Treasures of Japan, Series I, II. Catalogue of Art Objects Registered as National Treasures for the Year 1951–1952

Noguchi Yone: Ukiyo-e Primitives. Tokyo 1943

Oude Japansche Prentkunst (Catalogue door B. Modderman). S'Gravenhage 1938

Perzyński F.: Der Japanische Farbenholzschnitt. Berlin n. d.

Rumpf F.: Das Ise-Monogatari von 1806 und sein Einfluss auf die Buchillustration des XVII. Jahrhunderts in Japan; Inaugural Dissertation. Berlin 1931

Rumpf F.: Beiträge zur Geschichte der drei Holzschnittzeichnerschulen Torii, Okumura und Nishimura; Ostasiatische Zeitschrift N. F. 6. Jahrg. 1930, pp. 16–31, 87–101

Rumpf F.: Meister des Japanischen Farbenholzschnittes; Neues über ihr Leben und ihre Werke. Leipzig 1924

Sammlung Tony Straus-Negbaur: Japanische Farbholzschnitte des XVII. bis XIX. Jahrhunderts. Introduction by Curt Glaser, descriptions by Fritz Rumpf. Berlin 1928

Seidlitz W. von: Geschichte des Japanischen Farbholzschnittes. Dresden 1897, 1910, 1921, 1922, 1924, 1928

Shibui: Catalogue des estampes érotiques. Tokyo 1927

Strange E. F.: Japanese Illustrations; A History of the Art of Woodcutting and Colour-printing in Japan. London 1896, 1904

Takekoshi Y.: The Economic Aspects of the History of Civilisation of Japan. London 1930

Tokuno T.: Japanese Woodcutting and Woodcut Printing; Smithsonian Report, U. S. National Museum, Washington 1894, p. 221 ff.

Tsuda Noritake: Handbook of Japanese Art. Part I. A Brief History of Japanese Art. Part I. Guide to Temples and Museums. Tokyo 1935

APPENDIX

Sizes
Aiban: ca 33 × 22 cm.
Chuban: ca 25 × 16 cm.
Chu tanzaku: ca 37.5 × 12.5 cm.
Hoso-e: ca 30 × 15 cm.
Kakemono-e: ca 75 × 25 cm.
Naga-e (Hashirakake): ca 65 × 12.5 cm.
Oban: ca 37.5 × 25.5 cm.
Obosho: ca 51 × 37.5 cm.
O tanzaku: ca 37.5 × 17 cm.

Types
Tata-e: vertical picture
Yoko-e: horizontal picture
Byobu-e: picture to be pasted on a screen
Nobori-e: banner-picture
Uchiwa-e: fan-shaped picture
Sambukutsui: triptych

Technique
Sumi-e: black and white picture
Beni-e: saffron-red painted by hand on a black print: later, two-coloured print
Tan-e: cinnabar-red painted by hand on a black print
Urushi-e: black-lacquer painting on a print

Nishiki-e: brocade picture, i. e., multi-coloured print
Kappa-zuri-e: stencilled print

Themes
Bijin-e: picture of a beautiful girl
Binan-e: picture of a beautiful boy
Gigwa: humorous picture
Musha-e: picture of a battlefield
Nigao-e: portrait
Toba-e: caricature
Uki-e: picture with European perspective
Mivage-e: picture commemorating a journey
Shunga: spring-song, i. e., an erotic book

Other terms
Fude: brush
Ga: picture; painted by
Gako: painter
Hitsu: brush
Kaburo: a small girl as a servant to an oiran
Koto: lute
Mon: armour
Oiran: first prostitute of the house
Shamisen: guitar
Yujo: prostitute

COLOUR PLATES

九頭龍大權現

御本地神胎天

信州戸隱山

1

2

4

8

9

10

11

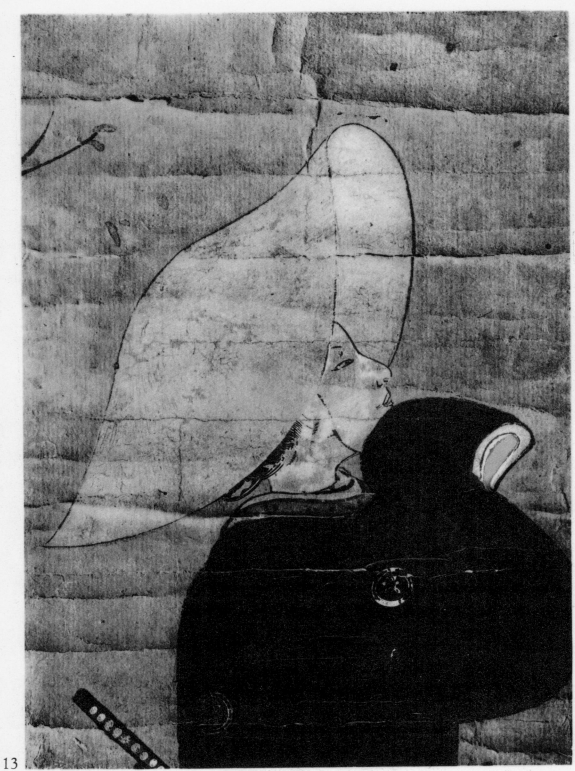

13

14

17

18

19

24

26

27

29

32

33

34

35

37

38

39

鬢頭二寸羹 女大喜

41

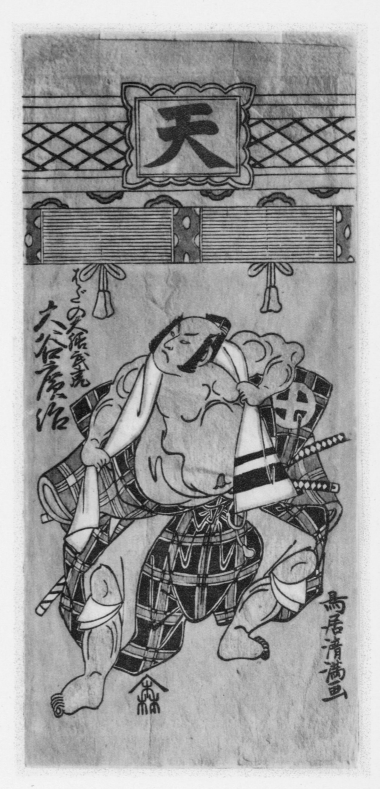

43

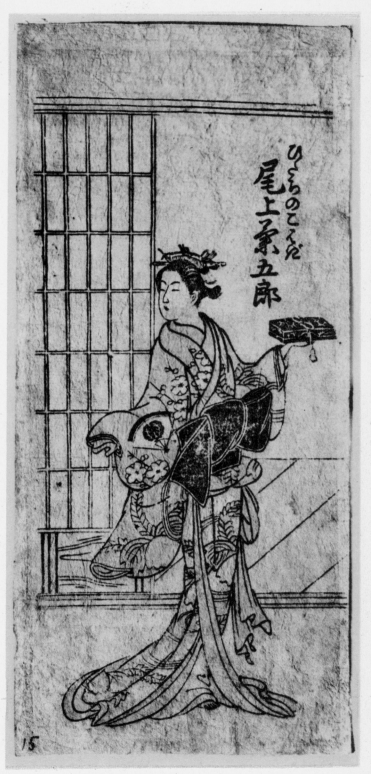

15

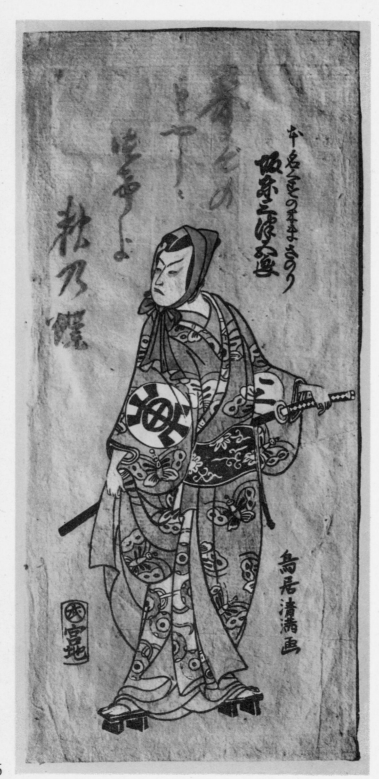

本名もとのままさのり
坂东三津五郎

春ごの
上下
生年よ
秋乃猩

鳥居清満画

國宮地

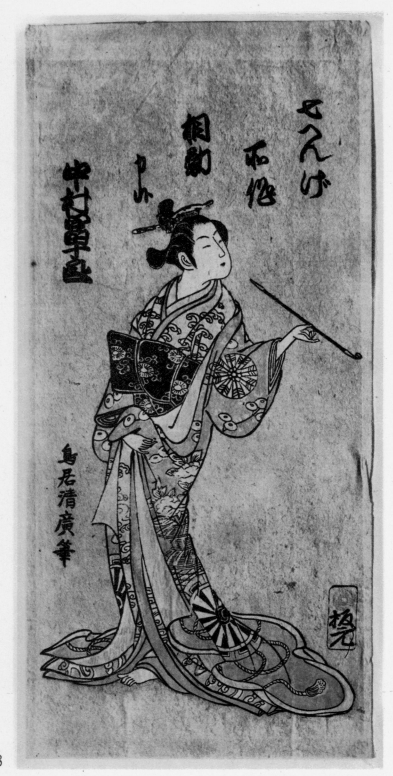

50